AN END TO CANCER?

A clear, concise layman's guide to the latest alternative approaches to the prevention and control of cancer, based on dietary reform and the use of Laetrile (vitamin B_{17}).

AN END
——TO——
CANCER?
The Nutritional Approach to its Prevention and Control

by

Leon Chaitow

N.D., D.O.

Member of the
British Naturopathic and Osteopathic Association

Illustrated by Bevil Roberts

THORSONS PUBLISHERS LIMITED
Wellingborough, Northamptonshire

First published 1978
Second Edition (revised, expanded and reset) 1983
Second Impression 1985

British Library Cataloguing in Publication Data

Chaitow, Leon
  An end to cancer? — 2nd ed
  1. Cancer — Nutritional aspects
  I. Title
  616.99'4'654   RC262

  ISBN 0-7225-0927-8

Printed and bound in Great Britain by
Whitstable Litho Ltd., Whitstable, Kent

CONTENTS

For ALKMINI, my wife.
With love and thanks.

Introduction

An end to cancer? Possibly.

A method for prevention of cancer? Probably.

An alternative way of looking at, and of treating cancer? Positively!

In this book the reader will be presented with a total biological approach to this disease. Not just one recommended substance, but a whole programme which fits together as a comprehensive method of combating cancer. The same factors and principles apply to both the prevention and treatment of cancer. They differ only in degree.

A refined, concentrated extract of a substance found in many foods will be recommended in the treatment of cancer. In its concentrated state it is called Laetrile. In its naturally occurring state it will be termed vitamin B17 (although it is not yet officially accepted as a vitamin).

In the words of one of Europe's foremost medical specialists on the use of Laetrile, Dr H. Moolenburgh:[1] 'I have been treating cancer patients for twenty-five years and introduced Laetrile four years ago. This was a turning point. For the first time I saw people who stayed alive in the late stages of cancer, against all expectations.

'Last year a man, hanging between his wife and his brother, sat down gasping for breath in my office. He was blue in the face and told me that lung cancer was killing him. It was too far gone for operation. Now, one year later, the man complains to me that he is "a little breathless" when he works too hard in his garden.'

I must stress that this approach to cancer must be understood as a combination of a dietetic regime, vitamin therapy (including Laetrile) enzyme and mineral therapy and psychotherapy. This will be repeated several times in order to overcome the tendency that exists to concentrate on one aspect of the treatment as the only vital or important aspect, ignoring the other requirements.

The purpose of this book is to introduce practitioners and patients to the use of Laetrile, and the diet and other supplements associated with it, in the treatment of cancer. The controversy as to the efficacy or otherwise of Laetrile in the treatment of cancer will eventually resolve itself. In the meantime the literature available on the subject is largely propagandist in nature, either hysterically against or enthusiastically for. I have attempted to synthesize from these works what appears to me to be relevant and valid. I will discuss the theory of how Laetrile achieves its effect, present the recommended method of administration and give a list of foods rich in vitamin B17 (amygdalin) which, theoretically, protects the body against the possibility of developing cancer. It will also be necessary to examine the alternative treatments currently available to victims of this disease.

It is important that the patient and family realize that Laetrile therapy is a broad approach to the patient's physical state. As well as the use of Laetrile, it is essential to alter the patient's diet radically and to include a range of other vitamins, minerals and enzymes. *Any attempt to simply use Laetrile as a treatment in its own right without these complementary adjuncts is certain to have little chance of success.*

Moolenburgh describes these methods as the 'gentle treatment of cancer', a phrase that describes perfectly his own caring, intuitive and yet intensely scientific (in the best sense of that much misused word) approach to his work.

In considering this form of treatment a patient might feel torn between what he would like to do and what is urged by orthodox medical advisers and family. It is possible to combine both forms of treatment, but only to a limited extent. Often patients who have had surgery, radiation, chemotherapy, or a combination of these approaches, will rebel against orthodox treatment and opt for the saner biological approach. In many such cases success is still achieved, but the best results are claimed for those whose bodies have not been subjected to this combination of methods. In certain cases, of course, surgery is necessary to save life (for example, in an acute bowel obstruction).

The relative value to the patient of radiation and chemotherapy will be discussed in a later chapter, but certainly the patient would do well to consider carefully the evidence available before deciding one way or the other whether to choose orthodox methods or those offered in this book. It does not add to the chance of success to 'back both horses'.

If this approach works, and on the evidence I have seen I believe that it can, then the chance of arresting cancer is at last available. More importantly, it leads to the possibility of the prevention of this scourge, by simple dietary methods. The antipathy and antagonism of organized medicine and its allies, the drug companies, are predictable. The reader will be led through the barrage of accusations, insinuations and slanders that have been hurled at the proponents of these methods in their battle to bring to the public attention the possibility of a natural cause (and cure) of cancer.

We shall be considering the circumstances in which cancer develops. In order to do this it is necessary to understand a number of processes which take place in the daily life of the human body. Some of these might seem too complicated for the layman to grasp. However, the importance of having a clear picture of the way in which the body achieves some of its remarkable processes will greatly assist the enquiring mind in its understanding of the methods and substances that this book suggests are vital to the maintenance and recovery of health.

If technical terms are not understood at first, then the reader may consult the glossary. Re-read sections and sentences so that what is being explained is clearly understood before pressing on to other sections of the chapter. If an idea is not grasped it might be tempting to skip it and move on; but this can only lead to confusion and the eventual misunderstanding of the explanations. The facts presented are supported by research and a great deal of work on the part of many dedicated people. In order to do justice to those efforts the reader is asked to make an effort in order to understand fully this revolutionary approach to the problem of cancer.

[1]Personal communication to the author, 1977.

1

How Cancer Starts

Cancer kills one person in five in Western Europe and North America, often in childhood.

But in spite of this high incidence the misconceptions and confusion that exist in the mind of the average individual regarding cancer are of enormous proportions. The fear and dread generated by the subject of this disease make it almost unmentionable. But this should not be so. It is the conclusion of the research and clinical experience discussed in this book that cancer is not only often controllable, once present in the human body, but that it is indeed preventable.

Present medical treatment of cancer is not aimed at causes but at symptoms. The attacks of surgeons, radiologists and physicians are on the tumour, the growth, the symptom. But the real causes lie deep in the way the body copes with the problems of self-healing and regeneration. The causes are not normally considered nor, in the main, is the general health of the patient. It is time to turn the focus of attention away from symptoms and towards the patient.

Cancer does not start from a single cell which suddenly alters its behaviour pattern, but from a whole series of changes in the affected tissue. A number of malignant cell changes occur more or less simultaneously within this field of diseased tissue. These localized structurally and functionally altered cells are surrounded by normal tissues. In many cases the minute tumours remain unchanged for months or even years.[1]

There is evidence[2] that such malignant cells appear frequently in the average individual but that they are often promptly destroyed by the body's defence mechanism. Nieper[3] points out that at post mortems of patients who died from non-cancerous causes some 22 per cent showed evidence of malignant tumours previously unnoticed.

Once a malignant tumour is well-established and growing rapidly it is said to metastasize. This means that germ cells break off from the tumour and travel through the blood or lymph channels to establish new sites for growth in distant areas of the body. Certainly this process occurs, but probably there are also secondary new growths which arise spontaneously as a result of the very factors that stimulated the first growth. These factors, external irritants, internal deficiencies and toxaemia, allow the proliferation of new sites for tumour development. Since there is a continued exposure to these factors it is logical to expect just such a spread of the disease.

Harris[4] states that not all malignant tumours produce metastases, and he goes on to say that a greater knowledge of the causes of metastasis would lead to an increase in control. It might be that more attention paid to the patient and his general state of well-being, and less attention to minutiae of cell behaviour, would give more knowledge of the 'why and wherefore' of metastases and of cancer as a whole.

However, whether or not tumours metastasize, the fact remains that treatment of the original tumour by surgery, or any other means, will only be dealing with a symptom and not with the cause of the disease. The whole body of the patient is ill and it must never be thought that the tumour is the disease. Only methods that correct the body's condition will provide a chance of real cure. If the body is able to destroy individual cells when they first show signs of abnormal growth, and if the body is able to re-establish control and destroy advanced malignant disease (this phenomenon — spontaneous remission — is discussed later in the chapter), then the ultimate aim of all those involved in treating cancer must be to create in the body just those conditions that allow such a healing effort to be made.

Sir Macfarlane Burnet[5], Nobel prize winner for his work in immunology, stated that there could be up to 100,000 cells in the body becoming cancerous each day. The average person's immunization system (defence mechanism) is so effective that it efficiently destroys these cancer cells. It is just such an aim that we are proposing, for all the cutting and irradiation and poisoning of cancer cells and tumours is only a battle against the symptoms of this disease. In no way do these methods help to create a healthy body. Only those that rebuild health, and which do not further devitalize an already sick body, will be successful and acceptable. We must recognize that cancer is not an invasion from outside the body: it is the result of changes within the normal body cells. This is a most important point and bears repeating and emphasizing. *Cancer results from changes within the normal body cells — it is not an invasion from outside, whatever irritants may induce the cells to change.* From this statement comes the important consideration that the basic cause of all the different types of cancer will be found to be within the body itself and not in the disease process or tumour.

Whilst there are known to exist hundreds of substances which irritate various body tissues and take part in the production of cancerous changes, these substances cannot be thought of as the major causes of the disease. Such substances are known as carcinogens, and what is important about them in our understanding of cancer is not that in some cases they appear to cause cancer but that in the majority of cases they do not. *For every cigarette smoker who contracts lung cancer at least ten smokers do not! The vital question is, why?*

A number of substances known to stimulate cancer in humans are discussed below. Unless otherwise indicated the information presented is derived from *Treatment of Inoperable Cancer* by W. Herberger, *Cancer: The Nature of the Problem* by Robert Harris and *World Without Cancer* by G.E. Griffin. These substances can be regarded as the 'final straw' or the last link in a chain which leads to cancer. They are not 'causes' in the absolute sense, since in millions of cases individuals do not respond to them by producing cancerous changes. Once we understand that the cause really lies in the underlying inability of the body to cope with these stimuli and to eradicate the malignant changes as they occur, we will have reached the point where we can start looking for the real cause of cancer.

It will then be seen that cancer's cause lies in a combination of factors including a slow intoxication of the body and its organs of regeneration, primarily the liver; a chemical imbalance between potassium and sodium, followed by the accumulation of tissue poisons and interference with cell respiration; a deficiency in proteolytic enzymes, which enable the body to neutralize cancer cells; and a deficiency in vitamin B_{17}, which has a specific anti-carcinogenic role. All these will be discussed in later chapters. Meanwhile let us consider briefly the environmental cancer-stimulating substances.

Carcinogens in Food

Many potential cancer-inducing substances occur in food additives — colouring, preservatives, etc. Although governmental agencies monitor these substances more carefully now than ever before, dangers still exist.

The research by Dr H. Druckrey into the effects of a known cancer-inducing dye, 'butter yellow', indicated that (1) the carcinogenic potential of such substances remains irreversible throughout life; (2) the effects of single doses are cumulative; (3) the effect depends upon the sum total of doses accumulated throughout life.

Coal tar derivatives are used as food dyes to make processed foods look more appealing. Many of these substances are potentially carcinogenic.

Substances used in the bleaching of foods (flour, white bread, etc.,) interfere with vital chemical processes. These are an advantage to the manufacturer for they give long shelf-life, but not to the consumer's health. The use of preservatives in vegetables and meat are also highly suspect as potential carcinogens.

A fungus, *aspergillus flavus,* and a toxin, *aflatoxin*, are found in certain moulds growing on peanuts. These can apparently produce liver and kidney cancer in animals, but it is not known whether there is any human susceptibility as a result of exposure to these moulds.

Saccharin and cyclamates, used as sweeteners, are suspected of inducing bladder cancer in animals.

Residues of pesticides have caused cancer in sheep, and no doubt would have similar cumulative effects in man.

Mouth cancer is common in areas of South East Asia where a leaf is chewed, in which tobacco and slaked lime are wrapped.

When fats are heated above 200°C (392°F) in food production certain chemical changes occur which result in the production of substances known to be carcinogenic to experimental animals. Frying is not recommended but if used as a means of food preparation, fats should never be re-used.

Insecticides containing arsenic and D.D.T. used on fruits and vegetables can induce cancer.

Smoked meat and fish often contain formaldehyde and creosote which are potentially carcinogenic.

The foods to avoid therefore are those produced, processed, preserved and presented in any way which involves these dubious methods.

The drinking of coffee should also be considered. During the roasting of coffee, matrol is produced. This substance inhibits cell respiration (a key factor in the change from a normal cell to a cancerous one). Long-term coffee drinking damages cell respiration and increases the danger of cancer, especially of the kidneys.

Cancer of the tongue, oesophagus and stomach is high among brewers, waiters, barmen, etc. Cancer of the oesophagus in particular has been linked to heavy drinking habits. Alcohol damages the body's main organ or regeneration, the liver. A condition of cirrhosis, which may result, is often a precursor to cancer.

Fluoridated water is now linked to a higher incidence of cancer.

Stanway[6] shows that there exists a connection between the Western diet, high in fat and low in roughage (fibre), and cancer of the colon. Not only is this condition almost unheard of amongst primitive people living on a low fat/high fibre diet but amongst American Seventh-Day Adventists, whose diet is vegetarian (i.e. almost always higher in fibre) the incidence of cancer of the colon is markedly lower than in the general population. There is no agreement as to the precise mechanism involved but it would seem that the slow passage of faeces through the colon, in the general population, allows greater exposure to the irritant substances which trigger cancer. This is a valid hypothesis but still neglects to stress that many people who are constipated and who have a fibreless, fat-laden diet do not contract bowel cancer. It is also worth pointing out that Seventh-Day Adventists and diet-conscious vegetarians, have a lower general incidence of all types of cancer. The vital factor is not the constipation, but the ability (or lack of it) of the body to withstand the irritant contact of faeces (or any other carcinogenic substance).

Carcinogens in Daily Use

Coal tar and petrochemical derivatives abound in carcinogenic substances. Many of these are used in toothpaste, hair oils, lipsticks and cosmetics. Various plastics and polymer films are known to be carcinogenic when embedded in animal tissue, e.g. cellophane, nylon, Teflon, Dacron, polyethylene, polystyrene and polyvinyl chloride. Carbon-tetrachloride used in cleaning processes is also highly carcinogenic.

One must also include the many atmospheric pollutants resulting from factory emissions, motor car exhausts, refinery discharges, aerosol sprays, and so on, in the list of carcinogenic substances. The link between tobacco smoking and cancer of the lung and bladder is too well documented to require consideration here.

Industrial Carcinogens

Workers in contact with any of the following substances are potentially at risk: tar, tar gas, pitch, asphalt, creosote, mineral oils, aniline dye, arsenic, copper, asbestos, nickel, plastics, radium, uranium, X-Rays.

A local form of lung cancer occurs in the miners of Erzebirge in Germany. At least half the miners were found to have lung cancer at autopsy, although many had died from other causes. The causative agent in their environment was thought to be either dust containing arsenic, or radioactivity. Whichever of these was the 'trigger' the fact that the other 50 per cent of miners at autopsy had no lung cancer is to me the really important one. Obviously virulent carcinogenic factors are at work in these miners and yet half of them displayed complete immunity to the irritants. Surely this is where research should have been concentrated and not on the half who did die of lung cancer.

Medical Carcinogens

All drugs are toxic to a greater or lesser degree. The medical use of drugs is a matter of the choice between relative evils, i.e. the effect of the disease weighed against the effect (short and long term) of the drug. This is the viewpoint of the orthodox profession. Those of us who see disease and the restoration of health from a different viewpoint would question the use of many such drugs. Irrespective of this view there do exist a number of carcinogenic substances in commonly used drugs.

Dr H. Gummel and Dr W. Lührs, German cancer researchers, are reported as having found sulphonamide drugs and antibiotics to be capable of accelerating the growth of tumours in animal experiments. Chloroform is known to be carcinogenic.

Medically induced cancers result from the therapeutic and diagnostic use of radiation (X-Rays, radioactive dyes, radioisotopes, etc).

The treatment of patients at radioactive spas or with radioactive mud can be regarded as involving the risk of cancer, if a pre-cancerous condition already exists in the patient.

Paraffin oil used in the treatment of constipation and other medical treatment is a potential hazard (similarly, all oil and coal derivatives).

The use of hormones in medical treatment is potentially carcinogenic. In this respect especial mention should be made of oestrogen. Contraceptive pills and other preparations containing this hormone must place the vulnerable patient at grave risk. The whole concept of hormone replacement therapy, so much in vogue at present, gives much cause for concern. The future will no doubt produce a re-thinking of the indiscriminate use of hormones but that will be too late for many.

Other Cancer-Inducing Agents

The radiation emitted by television sets is cumulatively damaging and colour sets are more harmful than black and white. A device has been patented in the U.S.A., which shows the viewer a mirror image of the screen, thereby shielding him from the X-Rays.

Certain virus particles are known to be active in some animal cancers and there is thought to be a link between such particles and some human cancers (for instance, Burkitt's lymphoma, cervical cancer in women). Even if a direct link is eventually established the question will need to be repeated: why only some and not others? The answer will as always be found in the body and its defence mechanism and not in the virus.

The trouble with cancer, states Dr Louis Goldman[7] is that we know many causes, but not *the* cause (if there is one). The reader may find difficulty in grasping the subtle difference between the underlying cause of cancer and a cancer-inducing substance (any of several hundred known carcinogens). In order for cancer to develop there has first to be an underlying pre-cancerous condition which allows whatever irritant happens to be in the patient's environment to trigger off the process.

A report in *The Times* was headlined 'Cancer: Chinese find cause in diet'. An intriguing title which proved once again that we must be on our guard when it is claimed that a 'cause' has been found. What the report indicated was that a particular type of cancer of the oesophagus was extremely prevalent in a region of China. Not only was it common in people but also in chickens. An environmental cause was sought. After much detective work a fungus that grows on a local vegetable pickle speciality was the prime suspect. It appeared that the chickens were fed scraps containing this fungus and therefore a common 'cause' was narrowed down.

Now, I do not dispute the accuracy of this finding. What is at issue is whether this is a cause or just one more trigger mechanism (just like cigarette smoke) which can only 'cause' cancer where a pre-cancerous condition exists. Otherwise one would anticipate that the entire population of Linhsien province would develop cancer of the gullet, along with all their chickens.

This is not the case, nor do all smokers develop lung cancer, though this does not mean that I am advocating the smoking habit or the consumption of pickled vegetables (with or without fungus).

A destructive habit such as smoking cannot be condoned, but there are too many healthy, smoking, octogenarians about to allow the habit to be labelled as a 'cause' of cancer. It plays its part in a chain of events, but the common denominator in all cancers is the condition of the body which allows it to grow. Therein lies the cause. It is nutritional considerations that provide the reasons for the underlying pre-cancerous state which is the true cause of cancer.

A connection between excessive radiation and the onset of cancer is well established. Kenneth Walker F.R.C.S.[8] points out that leukaemia very often occurs in people who have undergone extensive radiation treatment or who have been exposed to radiation in their work or via atomic explosions (e.g. Hiroshima). Leukaemia is a proliferation of white blood cells and ironically the treatment often consists of further radiation to cell-producing centres such as the marrow of the long bones. He quotes from Dr Bodley Scott:[9]

Leukaemia is undeniably a purposeless, progressive, unco-ordinated cellular proliferation, superfluous to the needs of the body, which continues after the causative stimulus has ceased to operate. As in other forms of cancer the abnormality seems to reside within the cells themselves.

He then goes on to point out the higher incidence of leukaemia in Hiroshima amongst the survivors of the atomic holocaust. Once again one must ask the question, why only some and not others? Many who were exposed to radiation did not develop abnormalities of this sort. The answer lies in the basic underlying resistance. The body is obviously irritated in just the same way as in the susceptible individual and yet the defence and healing mechanism does not allow the development of a cancerous change.

It is the apparent ability to control the early stages of cancer, triggered off by whichever irritant is active in the patient's environment, that should be the real concern of those who wish to understand the cancer problem.

In experiments carried out on volunteers in American prisons, cancer cells have been implanted in healthy bodies. In healthy subjects the cancer cells are destroyed, but in subjects already suffering from cancer the cells remain alive and active. In numerous similar experiments, workers such as Dr Druckrey and Dr D. Schmähl proved that implanted cancer tissue will be destroyed by a healthy body. Especially active in this process is the liver.

The body therefore has a natural defence mechanism against cancer cells which decreases as the general body efficiency diminishes into a state of generalized ill-health. Cancer is known to occur more frequently at times of lowered resistance, when the defence mechanism is either at a low ebb or under strain in other directions. Such vulnerable periods[2] occur during puberty, pre-menstrually, during certain infections, at the menopause, during periods of great anxiety and in the spring and autumn.

The Body's Defence Mechanism
Our attention must therefore be given to the body's defence mechanism so that such periods of vulnerability, combined with the influence of whatever cancer causing agent may be present, does not result in the disease becoming active. This will be considered in more detail when we come to the preventative measures that each and every one of us can introduce into our lives.

Normal body cells divide in a controlled manner, reproducing themselves (see illustration) to meet the needs of the body. For example, muscle tissue is constantly being broken down by exercise and use, and has to be replaced. In a precise and controlled manner the body manufactures just enough new cells to make up the loss. In a muscle that is being exercised to do more work the body will create new cells to make up the increased

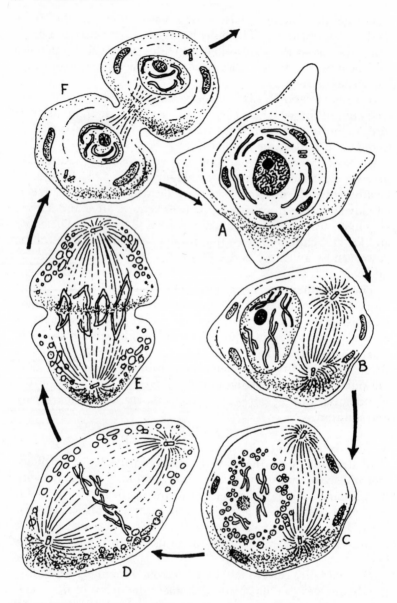

Fig. 1 Schematic diagram of mitosis of a cell showing the various stages leading to two new cells.

(A) Interphase (B) Prophase (C) End of Prophase (Prometaphase)
(D) Metaphase (E) Anaphase (F) Teleophase.

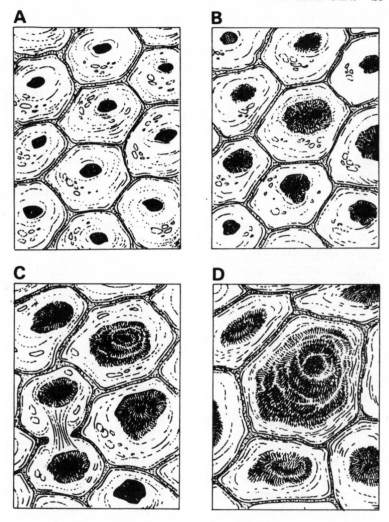

Fig. 2 Schematic diagram showing progressive deterioration of cells.

(A) Normal cells of the oesophagus (x 400). Note the uniformity of size and structure.

(B) The cells are showing signs of aberrant behaviour. Precancerous stage.

(C) Early cancerous stages are now evident. Note the division of a cell.

(D) Advanced cancerous changes. The cells have become undifferentiated.

size of muscle required to meet the new needs. The body starts the process and when enough cells have been created it slows down or stops the process. In cancer tissue, division and reproduction of new cells is unrestrained. The body appears to lose control and cannot stop the reproduction of new cells.

When a particular type of nerve cell (for there are different types of cells within each organ or tissue) reproduces itself it does so exactly. When cancer cells reproduce they may do so in a similar manner but often they produce cells that are quite different from the original tissue from which they have sprung (see illustration). This is known as anaplasia.

The rapid division of these rebellious cells usually leads to a swelling or tumour. This may of course interfere with the function of the tissues in which it grows or in adjacent tissues, for example, a growth in the oesophagus would be expected to interfere with swallowing.

Whilst cell division in cancer cells is usually more rapid than in normal tissue this is not by any means as rapid as it might be. For example, cell division in a growing baby is more rapid than in most tumours. The difference is that in the baby the growth, and therefore the rate, of cell division is controlled and in the tumour it is not. Evidence of an active tumour would be gained by the presence of a swelling containing cells which microscopically displayed changes in their architectural structure.

As has been indicated, many malignant changes take place in body cells which never develop: the body contains the growth. There is evidence,[4] for example, that between 30 and 40 per cent of men over fifty have cancer cells in their prostate glands. The majority of these never develop into a malignant tumour in this organ. Wilkinson[5] mentions a series of a thousand thyroid glands examined at post mortem. The patients in all these cases had died of causes unrelated to cancer, which was not apparent in any of them. Over 50 per cent were found to contain malignant nodules.

The general changes that have taken place in the body prior to the onset of the first major symptoms of cancer are early warnings, and were we able to recognize these more clearly, then the development of malignancies would be relatively easy to prevent.

Cancer can arise at a single focal point but more often there are a multitude of sites in the affected tissue where atypical cells

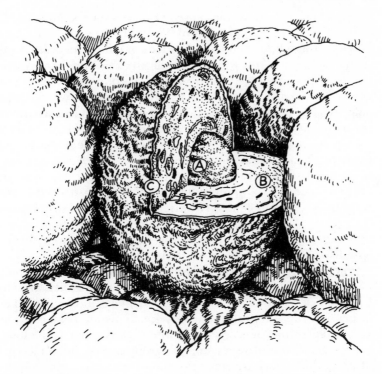

Fig. 3 Normal Cell.
The cutaway section shows (A) The nucleus (B) The protoplasm and
(C) The cell membrane.

(cells that have changed in shape or function) abound. Thus,
logically, the predisposing factors have created a soil in which
many malignant cells will grow.

There are many indirect causes that lead to the damage of
cells prior to cancerous changes occurring. The respiration of
the cell becomes altered and instead of deriving energy in the
normal manner from oxygen, a process called glycolysis takes
place. This is a fermentation process whereby sugar is turned
into lactic acid. The destruction of the process of respiration is
seen as the essence of the change from a normal cell to an abnormal fermenting cell (the cancer cell).

There are many theories as to what happens to make cells apparently go berserk in this way. Explanations of this extremely
complicated process requires the reader to be aware of a
number of facts which will help in the understanding of the pro-

blem. In our search for the cause of cancer we must turn our attention to the very beginning of life itself.

The human body is made up of tens of billions of cells. A cell is the smallest unit which has all the features of a living creature. A cell grows, feeds, moves, reproduces, excretes and reacts to external factors. For practical purposes we can consider cells as the bricks that build up the body. Cells are made up of a jelly-like substance, known as protoplasm, contained within a membrane or skin. In each cell there exists one (sometimes more than one) nucleus. It is the nucleus which contains the instructions relating to the particular cell's function and which enables it to reproduce itself, when instructed by the body to do so. Cells come in a variety of shapes and sizes depending on their particular function. When a great number of cells of a particular type are grouped together in order to perform a specific function they form what are called 'tissues'.

The various types of body tissues such as muscle, nerves, etc, comprise groups of cells of their particular type which are virtually stuck together by a complex chemical interaction. The larger and more complicated body functions are performed by very large groups of cells formed into organs, such as the liver, heart, etc. These organs comprise groupings of different types of cells which work together to produce the effect required by the body (for example, production of digestive juice, pumping of blood, etc).

When an embryo is starting to grow in the mother's womb it consists of what are known as primitive undifferentiated cells. These cells are rapidly reproducing themselves but do not as yet represent any particular type of tissue. It is only as time passes that 'differentiated' cells appear. That is to say, cells which have become different from the others and which will form a unique tissue or organ. Some cells (for example, neurons or nerve cells) gradually lose the ability to reproduce themselves by division while others, such as the stem cell, retain this ability throughout life.

When cells containing the same chromosomes (inherited coded material) begin to manufacture different proteins they are said to be differentiating. This process is controlled by a variety of chemical messengers which operate between and inside the cells.[10] Tumours which consist of cells that closely resemble the tissues in which they are growing are said to be made up of well-differentiated cells and are considered to be relatively innocent

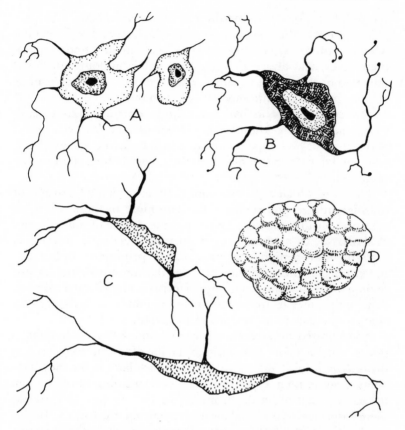

Fig. 4 Various types of nerve cells which will each form a specialized tissue structure.
(A) The immature microglia cell (B) The mature inactive cell
(C) Rod cells (D) Lattice cell.

or benign.[1] Tissues involved in a healing process[11] may encourage the onset of malignancy in the newly formed cells. Primary carcinoma of the liver sometimes occurs in cases of cirrhosis and arise from the liver cells which are endeavouring to regenerate.

The speed at which cells can divide and reproduce themselves varies. Some can be replaced extremely rapidly when wear and tear occur in, for example, the intestines. Other situations, such as the healing of a skin wound, produces a different picture. When a cut is healing there is at first a very rapid division of cells to repair the wound. This is followed by a slowing down of the process until normal tissue has been reformed.

The needs of the body are therefore the factors that determine when, and at what speed, cells will divide and replace themselves, and above all when they will stop doing so. For if they do not stop, then we have what is known as a neoplasm or a 'new growth', commonly called a tumour.

The precise way in which the body instructs cells to stop reproducing is not known. A number of theories exist and a description of how this important control may be achieved will be given later when we introduce the theory behind the Laetrile treatment.

Tumours which are malignant contain a high proportion of undifferentiated embryonic cells. The more of these primitive cells present in a tumour the greater the degree of malignancy. When tissue is examined to determine whether a tumour is malignant or benign, the presence of primitive, undifferentiated cells, is taken to indicate that the tumour or tissues are malignant.[12] This has led many scientists and medical experts to believe that it is in the study of these embryonic cells that the clues to the causes of cancer are to be found.

A celebrated nineteenth century doctor, Julius Cohnheim,[13] put forward a theory that early in the life of the embryo some of the cells go into a 'rest' phase. When much later in life they suddenly resume their rapid growth they form tumours. Another theory was that of Dr A. Fromme. In 1953 he put forward the theory that embryonic cells were responsible for cancer. In the early stages of the embryo's development in the mother's womb three layers of cells are found. These are the ectoderm, which later differentiates into the skin, the nervous system and the sense organs; the mesoderm, which later becomes the muscles, heart, spleen, lymphatic tissue, blood vessels, connective tissue and the organs of excretion; and the endoderm, which becomes the digestive canal.[2] Fromme maintained that many of the cells which make up the various organs and tissues that derive from the mesoderm have never undergone differentiation and are therefore still 'embryonic cells'.

The ability of the body to deal with injury, infection, physical or chemical damage or ageing depends on those organs and systems which derive from the mesoderm. This has been termed the Reticulo Endothelial System (R.E.S.) and it provides the possibility, through its component cells, for tissue regeneration and therefore for life itself. Since all tumours consist, at least in part, of connective tissue, blood vessels and lymphatic structures, Fromme believed that any pre-cancerous condition was to be found in these areas of the body.

Spontaneous Remission

The rare, but nevertheless vitally important, phenomenon known as spontaneous remission of cancer should be mentioned at this point. Advanced cases of malignant cancer have been known to heal spontaneously and completely. It is the R.E.S. that deals with all healing and it is important that we remember this possibility as we consider the subject of cancer.

This phenomenon is not as rare as one might imagine. One of Britain's leading research scientists into cancer, Robert Harris,[4] quotes the following list of sites where cancer has spontaneously regressed (i.e. disappears for no obvious external reason): bladder; breast; colon/rectum; kidney; mouth; ovary; uterus; lung; stomach and pancreas. He quotes an investigation of six hundred claims of such spontaneous remissions by Everson and Cole. These were examined in minute detail and forty-seven were found to be proved beyond doubt. If this sort of number of 'self-cures' is expanded to take account of the entire world population of cancer sufferers then the probability exists that thousands of such remissions occur. The aim of the combined therapy advocated in this book is to create just those conditions required by the body to enable it to successfully combat the malignant growth within it.

Herberger makes a clear distinction between what he calls spontaneous cures, which occur when no medical treatment has been carried out at all and where no other illness or relevant influence has been present, and natural healing which takes place when a simultaneous disease (fever or infection) was involved in bringing about the liquidation of the tumour. Spontaneous cures, he says, are rare, but natural healing of tumours has been observed more often.

Davidson[14] states that although unusual, spontaneous remission is well documented. He refers to the little-known immunilogical processes which may protect the patient against the spread of cancer. Nutritional factors, he considers, may contribute to this protection.

Oestrogen

In 1902 a theory was put forward as to the cause of cancer by

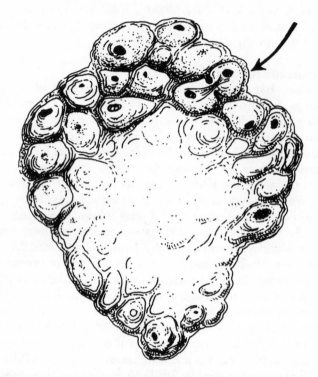

Fig. 5 Drawing of a minute human embryo (107 cells) showing the undifferentiated trophoblast cells. These are indistinguishable from the undifferentiated cells found in malignant tissue. Note cell (arrowed) where mitosis (cell division) is taking place.

Professor Beard of Edinburgh University. Being an embryologist his studies had led him to a study of primitive (undifferentiated) cells and their relationship to cancer. He maintained that certain cells, called trophoblasts, which were part of the normal mechanism for attaching the embryo to the wall of the mother's uterus, were in later life largely responsible for cancer.

A complicated process involving primitive undifferentiated cells and the hormone oestrogen takes place in the formation of the human embryo and the placenta (the sack in which the unborn baby develops inside the mother). It is now known that an enormous number of these primitive cells remain present in the body as it develops and matures. Many are located in the ovaries or the testes and serve a function in creating material for reproduction. There are, however, throughout the body many such cells and it is thought that they take part in any process of healing or regeneration. This would appear to happen frequently in normal individuals and to be a controlled process. That is to say, whenever healing of damaged or irritated tissues takes place, these cells are activated by the body and when healing is complete the body is able to 'switch off' the process of new tissue growth.

Oestrogen is commonly thought of as a female sex-hormone and yet it appears in many of the body processes in both sexes. It is thought to be involved in triggering the re-activation of primitive (undifferentiated) cells in situations requiring new cell growth for body repair. An overabundance of oestrogen and other hormones would therefore be potentially harmful, in the sense that they would favour the development of a cancerous condition (through over-stimulation of undifferentiated cells).

This must raise serious doubts as to the wisdom of women taking a contraceptive pill containing oestrogen and of the use of this and other hormones in animals that are used for human consumption. Cancer *in situ* can exist for many years in a quiescent state before active invasion begins. Very few women have taken oral contraceptives for long enough to provide substantial evidence one way or the other. It will need twenty to thirty years to show the real effects on the users.

If oestrogen activity stimulates the undifferentiated cells into activity the body will attempt to stop this process by use of enzymes and white blood cells. If this is successful, and the sudden new growth is contained, it might well leave a benign tumour or polyp at the site of the battle.[15] If it fails to switch off the process, cancer results. Obviously the ability of the body to accomplish this control will become strained if (a) there exists a constant degree of irritation or injury to tissues, such as in cigarette smoking, or (b) the specialized substances that are used by the body to stop this process of cell reproduction become either diminished in potency or quantity, so that growth becomes unrestrained and cancer develops.

In medical experiments on animals it has been found that one substance can reinforce the effects of another substance in order to 'cause' cancer. Berenblum painted the skin of mice with a weak solution of benzpyrene. Three out of 102 animals developed skin cancer. He then painted another group of mice with benzpyrene followed by an application of croton oil. Out of the eighty-three animals thus treated thirty-six developed tumours. Among 106 animals exposed to croton oil alone, only one developed cancer. This type of experiment leads researchers to talk of substances which 'initiate' cancer and the whole process is called co-carcinogenesis.

Does the reader believe that this will lead to a better understanding of the causes of cancer? Only, I suggest, if the emphasis is placed on why the other forty-seven mice, in the main experiment, did not develop cancer. I repeat the importance of concentrating attention on health and not on disease. The cause of cancer lies in the state of health of the body (mouse or human) and not in the substances that trigger, initiate or promote the disease.

It should now be clear that the concentration, by researchers, on irritant substances, will never lead to the eradication of cancer. There are enormous numbers of such irritants which occur both naturally (e.g. ultraviolet light from the sun) and as a result of civilized life. The cause and therefore the prevention and possible cure of cancer lies with the understanding of the mechanism whereby the body exercises control of the healing process that are triggered off by these irritants.

Enzymes

Among the many chemical processes that take place in the body there exist a whole range of substances known as enzymes. An enzyme is a catalytic substance (a catalyst is something that has the power to alter the speed of a chemical reaction but does not change as a result of the process) which has a specific role to play in the numerous processes of the body. There are over seventy different enzymes, each with its own particular job to do. We are concerned with enzymes produced by the pancreas (a large gland which lies at the back of the upper abdominal area which produces a number of digestive juices, enzymes and the hormone insulin) as inactive zymogens.

This means that these enzymes are not active until they come into contact with an appropriate chemical substance. The enzymes of particular interest to us in this study are trypsin and chymo-trypsin, as well as to a lesser extent, the other pancreatic enzymes.

The primitive trophoblast cell, which has been stimulated to activity as part of a healing process, has a coat of protein material which protects it from attack by the body's normal defence mechanism, i.e. the white blood cells (lymphocytes,

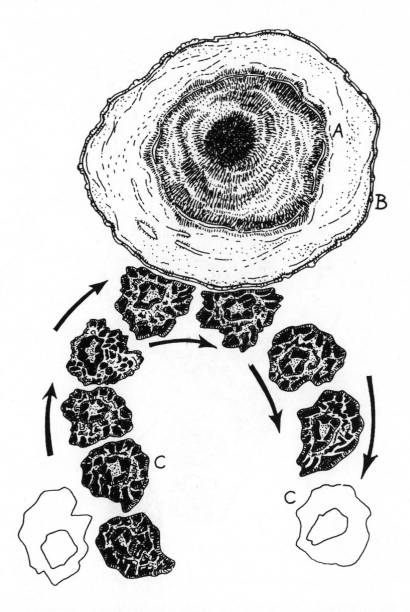

Fig. 6 Schematic diagram showing (A) Cancerous cell being protected by (B) Protein shield from (C) White blood cells (leukocytes, phagocytes, etc.).

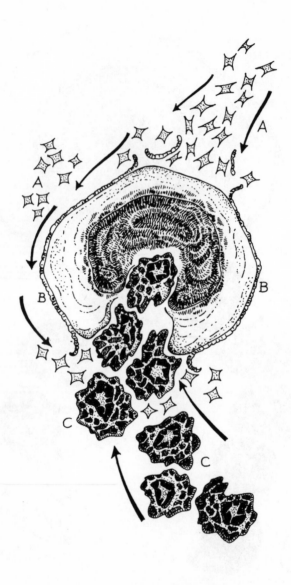

Fig. 7 Schematic diagram showing (A) Proteolytic (protein digesting) enzymes destroying the protective shield of (B) The cancer cell which can now be successfully attacked by (C) White blood cells (leukocytes, phagocytes, etc.).

leukocytes, monocytes). These white blood cells are normally active in destroying invading foreign micro-organisms and it would seem logical that if cancer cells were foreign to the body then the white blood cells would attack and destroy them. It is the protein coating of the trophoblast cell that by its electrostatic charge protects these cells from the white blood cells. The active cancer cell has just such a protective coat which has to be over-come by the body if it is to destroy the tumour. The enzymes produced by the pancreas are the body's method of controlling the proliferation of the trophoblasts. These enzymes are ac-tivated by the protein coat of the trophoblast which they digest, allowing the white blood cells to destroy the cell.

We have mentioned that the trophoblast cells are actively in-volved in the development of the embryo and the placenta. If the combination of pancreatic enzymes and white blood cells can destroy cancer cells (which are trophoblast cells activated later in life) then the question arises as to why the enzymes pro-duced by the mother's pancreas do not check the normal pro-liferation of these cells. A number of theories exist, but as yet no conclusive answer is available. The body must produce some blocking agent which prevents this enzyme action. The trophoblast cells in the embryo develop and divide up to about the eighth week of pregnancy when the baby's pancreas starts functioning.

To summarize the trophoblast theory of cancer:
1. Primitive trophoblast cells exist in all parts of the body.
2. These cells take an active part in the healing and regenera-tion of tissues.
3. The body can prevent 'overhealing' by a combination of pancreatic enzymes and white blood cells.

The critical importance of an adequate concentration of these pancreatic enzymes now becomes apparent.

The pancreas may fail to produce an adequate supply of en-zymes or the diet might include so much of the foods (high pro-tein) which require these pancreatic enzymes for their diges-tion, that not sufficient is left for the attack on proliferating cells. On the other hand the pancreas may produce adequate enzymes and yet, because of a deficiency of vitamins in the diet, the efficiency of these enzymes is diminished. These vitamins are known as co-enzymes and without them the activity of the enzymes is incomplete.

There exist in the body substances which prevent protein-digesting enzymes from actually digesting the healthy body cells. In a state of ill-health the body may produce too much of these anti-enzyme substances and this could prevent enzymes from working normally when attacking cancer cells. Any chronic deficiency of mineral substances which take part in the activation of enzymes may also result in a poor enzyme attack on cancer cells.

For all these reasons the body may be hampered in its efforts to control the explosion of cell growth that occurs in cancer.

In order to assist the body in its attempt to destroy tumours, extra enzymes are recommended. Richardson, Kelley and other American workers use enzymes, active in the breakdown of protein, which are derived from animal pancreatic tissue. Nieper, Moolenburgh and other European and American workers advise the use of bromelaine. This is an enzyme, derived from the pineapple plant, which is effective in destroying the protective protein 'coat' of the cancer cell. Details will be given in the chapter dealing with supplements to be used with the diet.

The body has, however, another method of controlling unwanted cell proliferation. This involves the substance now known as Laetrile.

[1] J. Hoag, W. Cole, S. Bradford, *Osteopathic Medicine*, McGraw Hill, 1969.

[2] W. Herberger, *Treatment of Inoperable Cancer*, John Wright and Son, 1965.

[3] H. Nieper, 'Changes and Prospects in Medical Treatment of Cancer', *Medizin*, 1976.

[4] R. Harris, *Cancer: The Nature of the Problem*, Penguin, 1976.

[5] J. Wilkinson, *The Conquest of Cancer*, Hart-Davis MacGibbon, 1973.

[6] A. Stanway, *Taking the Rough with the Smooth*, Souvenir Press, 1976.

[7] Louis Goldman, *When Doctors Disagree*, Hamilton, 1973.

[8] K. Walker, *The Story of Blood*, Herbert Jenkins, 1958.

[9] R. Bodley Scott, *Medical Society Transactions*, LXXXIII.

[10] *Gray's Anatomy*, 35th edition, Longman, 1973.

[11] *Short's Practice of Surgery*, 16th edition, H.K. Lewis, 1975.

[12] H.C. Elliot, *Text Book of Neuroanatomy*, Lippincott, 1969.

[13] *Blakiston's New Gould Medical Dictionary*, McGraw Hill, 1956.

[14] Sir Stanley Davidson, R. Passmore, J.F. Brock and A. Truswell, *Human Nutrition and Dietetics*, 6th edition, Churchill Livingstone, 1975.

[15] G.E. Griffin, *World Without Cancer*, American Media, 1976.

2

Laetrile and Cancer

Amygdalin was originally extracted from bitter almonds. Its name derives from the tree which produces the bitter almond, *Prunus amygdalus*. It is one of the nitrilosides and occurs naturally in a great many foods and plants. It has also been given a provisional place in the group of vitamins forming the B-complex, as vitamin B_{17}. A concentrated extract of this substance has been named Laetrile.

The name Laetrile was given to an extract derived from apricot kernels by the researcher who isolated the crystalline form of this substance, Ernst Krebs Ph.D. To avoid confusion I shall refer only to Laetrile, the concentrated form of amygdalin (vitamin B_{17}). In the presence of water the three constituents of Laetrile can be separated by an enzyme to produce glucose (sugar), benzaldehyde (a substance comprising some 80 per cent of the Laetrile compound) and hydrocyanic acid, a poison. These last two substances are synergistic, which means that although individually poisonous they are infinitely more powerful when combined. The enzyme which can split the Laetrile compound is beta-glucuronidase (also known as glucosidase or emulsin) which occurs in great quantities in and around cancer cells. When the combined substances are released by this enzyme they act to destroy cancer cells. However, when they come into contact with normal cells some of which also contain beta-glucuronidase, the released poisons are neutralized by yet another enzyme, rhodanese, (thiosulphate transulphurase).

Laetrile therefore contains powerful cancer-destroying agents which are only released when in contact with an enzyme that is found mainly in cancer cells. The body protects normal cells from damage by neutralizing these substances with another enzyme found throughout the body, but not in cancer cells.

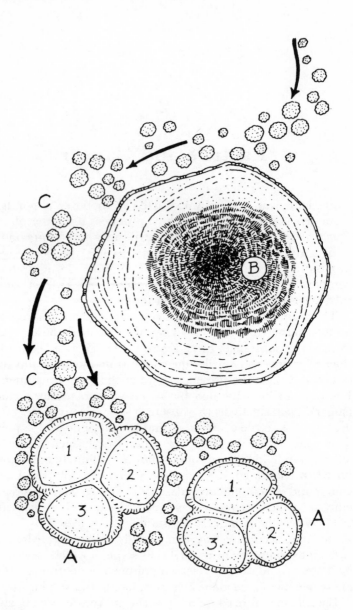

Fig. 8 Schematic diagram showing (A) Laetrile compound arriving in the vicinity of (B) Cancer cell around which lies the enzyme (C) Beta-glucuronidase, which splits Laetrile into its components (1) Sugar (2) Benzaldehyde (3) Hydrocyanic acid.

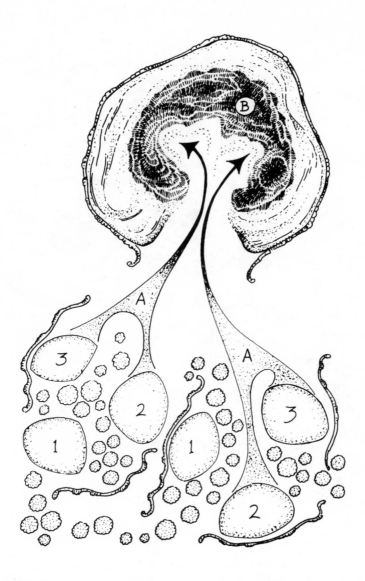

Fig. 9 Schematic diagram showing (A) Benzaldehyde (2) and Hydro-cyanic acid (3) combining synergistically to attack and destroy (B) Cancer cell.

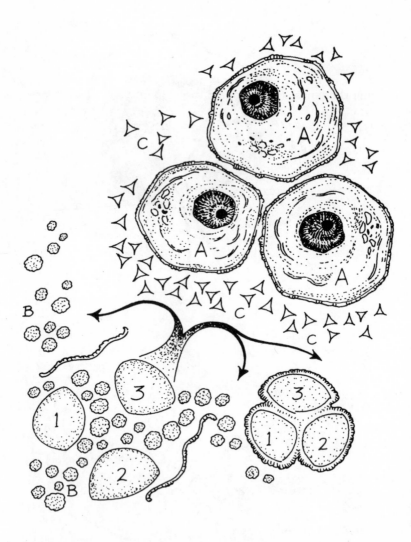

Fig. 10 Schematic diagram showing (A) Normal cells around which occur small quantities of (B) the enzyme Beta-glucuronidase which splits Laetrile into its components (1) Sugar (2) Benzaldehyde and (3) Hydrocyanic acid. These cells are protected from the potentially poisonous effect of the cyanide by another enzyme (C) Rhodinase which is found in all normal tissue but not in cancerous tissue.

Nieper states that Laetrile is more effective against cancer cells when they are duplicating slowly and when the cells' respiration is high (early stages of malignancy). In advanced stages, therapy utilizing minerals, etc., should be used to enhance Laetrile activity.

When Laetrile is split into its component substances and these are in contact with normal (non-cancerous) tissues, the enzyme rhodanese (thiosulphate transulphurase), which is present in normal tissues, converts the cyanide component into a substance useful to the body, thiocyanate. This takes part in the body's self-regulation of blood-pressure. Thiocyanate is also used by the body in the production of vitamin B_{12} (cyanocabolamine), another vital vitamin, which has cyanide as an ingredient. The other component of Laetrile, benzaldehyde, when in contact with normal body cells, is rapidly converted into a substance with antiseptic and pain killing properties, benzoic acid.

The basic research and development of Laetrile was the work of Ernst Krebs Jr. Many other researchers and doctors have since worked to produce a system which enables the most advantageous use to be made of this discovery. Laetrile is found to work most effectively in the treatment of existing cancer, when combined with a strict diet as well as with enzymes and mineral and vitamin supplements. Details will be given of these methods later. At this stage, however, emphasis must be placed on the importance of realizing that Laetrile on its own, though helpful, offers only a limited chance of controlling an advanced, proliferating, cancerous process. By this stage the patient's options are very limited indeed and a total approach must be made not just to destroy the cancer process but to begin to rebuild the ravaged body's health. Thus any criticism of Laetrile, based on tests done independently of the 'total' approach must be treated with scepticism.

It must be stated that some patients will not recover, even with a dedicated application of the approach advocated in this book. Damage to the organs of repair may be too far advanced or the spread of the cancer may be so prolific as to make the task of the body too great. Nevertheless the improvement in the quality of life that is possible is worth working for.

Moolenburgh[1] puts it well when he says 'a lot of patients with hopeless cancer feel better, have less pain and live longer than I would have expected. And some cases live on and on and on, which could not be expected at all. I did not see that sort of patient before Laetrile.'

The California Medical Association who investigated Laetrile and were critical of its value as an anti-cancer substance (they did not use the comprehensive approach advocated by this book) published a report which included this phrase[2]: 'All of the physicians whose patients were reviewed spoke of an increase in the sense of well being and appetite, gain in weight and decrease in pain.'

In Indonesia several hundred cases of breast cancer[1] have been treated using a nitriloside derived from cassava. A total dietetic approach was not included in this therapeutic approach. No side effects were noted apart from transient dizziness, which quickly passed. The report mentions improvement in eating and sleeping, less pain, feeling of well-being, increase in weight and reduction in tumour size. In some cases the tumour disappeared. Results were better in cases not previously treated with surgery or radiation.

The majority of patients seeking advice and treatment with Laetrile have already been treated surgically or with radiation or chemotherapy. Most of them have been classified as terminal cases, or in other words, beyond hope of recovery. At this stage of the disease the anticipated five year survival rate under orthodox care is less than one in a thousand patients, that is, under 1/10 of 1 per cent.

Figures prepared by those physicians who have been working with Laetrile long enough to assess a five year survival rate show that, of these terminal patients with an anticipated survival rate of less than 1/10 of 1 per cent, who were treated with the comprehensive approach, incorporating Laetrile, there is approximately a 15 per cent survival rate. A number of physicians who have been using Laetrile for a shorter time (three or four years) have shown a higher percentage than 15 per cent surviving in good health.

Patients treated with Laetrile therapy, in whom there has been no metastasis, are estimated[4] to enjoy an 80 per cent long-term survival rate. These figures are improved in cases where no damage to vital organs has been occasioned either by the disease or by chemical or radiation therapy. Griffin gives a figure of 28 per cent anticipation of five year survival if these patients undergo orthodox therapy.

Now all statistics are suspect and capable of manipulation.

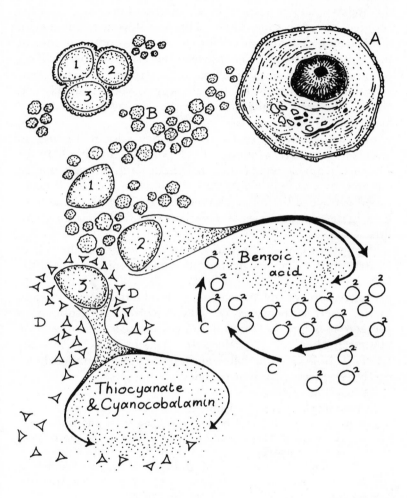

Fig. 11 Schematic diagram showing in the vicinity of (A) Normal cells, the potentially dangerous components of Laetrile, which having been released by (B) Beta-glucuronidase are changed into harmless substances as follows: Benzaldehyde (2) reacts with oxygen (C) to produce Benzoic acid, a natural pain killer; Hydrocyanic acid (3) reacts with the enzyme Rhodanese (D) to produce Thiocyanate which assists the body in regulating blood pressure. The remainder is used by the body to produce Cyanocobalamin (vitamin B_{12}).

This fact will be discussed further when we consider the orthodox treatment of cancer in a later chapter. The only other method available is to quote case histories. These are often discounted as being 'anecdotal'. This is a favourite method of disregarding case histories that the sceptic has not examined at first hand. The figures and case histories presented by Richardson in *Laetrile Case Histories* are packed with supportive material. Given time the case for Laetrile therapy will be statistically and clinically proved. In the meantime the facts as presented must give even the sceptic pause.

Laetrile is non-toxic. Even its critics seldom attempt to criticize it on the grounds of its possible toxicity. All the evidence available points to Laetrile in its natural form being an essential part of man's diet. Amygdalin (Laetrile) is a concentrated extract of the bitter almond and has been listed as non-toxic in the pharmocopoeias of various countries for over a hundred years.

We will deal with the various attacks made on the use of Laetrile in the chapter which deals with the controversy in the U.S.A.

One researcher who appears to be developing ideas very close to the Laetrile theory is Dr David Rubin. Dr Rubin is a surgeon at Beilinson Hospital and does cancer research at the Hadassah Hospital, Jerusalem. In an issue of the *West Sussex Gazette* in June 1977 the following report appeared under the title 'New cancer treatment revealed':

> In layman's language, Dr Rubin makes up a package containing a poison in such a way that normal cells pass it on unopened, as it were, but when it reaches a cancer cell the package is ripped open, the poison is released and the cell is killed.
>
> It was too early to make claims which might raise false hopes, he said, but added that all four patients on whom he had tried the treatment had shown dramatic improvements.
>
> His discovery came about when he started to think what was specific to cancer cells and in certain cancer cells he found a large amount of an enzyme Beta-glucuronidase, much more than in normal cells.
>
> One of the properties of enzymes is that they will split certain molecules, and this particular one will separate Mandelo-nitrille [author's note: Mandelo-nitrille is benzaldehyde and cyanide in combination] from Beta-D-glucuronide.
>
> The first of these two substances is toxic, but when the two are

combined they form a completely harmless substance.

Dr Rubin injects this substance into the patient and when it reacts with a normal cell nothing happens, the package passes on untouched until it reaches a cancer cell.

Here the enzyme immediately splits the package open, the toxic Mandelo-nitrille is released and the cancer cell dies.

At present his treatment is not effective against any cancer. It will not, for example, treat leukaemia 'but', he told his audience, 'leukaemia cells have high activity of a different enzyme so that the same method might be available, using different substances'.

He was asked about treating further patients, but he said that this was not yet possible. The amount of the substance used for treatment, which he calls DMBG, is only enough for his present patients.

At the moment the DMBG is produced from goats, which limits the output, but on his return to Israel his first priority will be to find a way of synthesizing it in the laboratory.

The resemblance between the theory mentioned in this report and the way in which Laetrile is known to work is obvious. The report does not mention a total approach to the patient. It is presented as a potential cure for cancer. Indeed it is apparently yet another attack on the symptoms with little or no thought for the causes of the disease.

In his book *Laetrile Case Histories* Dr John Richardson quotes from a report to the Ministry of Health in Israel made by Dr Rubin, who gives an enthusiastic account of work he had witnessed in the U.S.A. on cancer using Laetrile. This report was dated October 1976.

It is important to maintain a broad view regarding the treatment of cancer. From the description of the action of Laetrile it would be understandable were anyone to think that Laetrile alone would be adequate in treating cancer. The whole body is ill and out of balance, chemically, once cancer has manifested itself. No single approach or substance can restore normality. The body must be rebuilt dietetically. The pancreatic enzymes must be replaced, if deficient (which they usually are in cancerous patients). All the vitamins and minerals must be present in the diet and some given as supplements. Laetrile (vitamin B_{17}) must be given in large doses until the disease begins to yield. All these methods and others involving the patient's mental attitude as well as avoiding obvious irritants (for example, tobacco smoke) must be instituted.

It is now known that copper is eliminated from cancer cells and that replacement of this is important in treatment. This is known as copper retrotransport. The effect of copper replacement is to slow down the rate at which the cell 'breathes'. This is extremely important to the success of Laetrile therapy, since it is when cell division is relatively slow that Laetrile is most effective against cancer cells.

[1] Personal communication to the author.
[2] Report of the Cancer Commission of California Medical Association, 1953.
[3] 'One Year's Experience of Treating Breast Tumours with SPP Cassava', *Medica*, Vol 1, No 1, August 1976.
[4] McNaughton Foundation data submitted to F.D.A., 1970, quoted by J.A. Richardson, *Laetrile Case Histories*, American Media, 1977.

3

Diet and Cancer

The evidence connecting nutrition with the development of cancer is overwhelming. The success, or otherwise, in treating cancer is directly linked to the patient's ability to radically alter the diet, and to stick to the changes.

Many eminent nutritionists such as Sir Robert McCarrison, Dr M. Bircher-Benner and Dr W. Herberger insist that cancerous disease is largely a result of lifelong dietary faults, aggravated by other environmental factors. Bircher-Benner after a lifetime of research stated[1] 'I myself am convinced that cancer arises from the soil of disordered living, especially through disordered nutrition.' Hoffman[2] did a great deal of research into cancer and came to two main conclusions: (a) cancer is a disease of the whole organism; (b) deep-seated nutritional influences must be regarded as causal factors.

Dr Werner Kollath[3] has showed that a diet of poor nutritional value can lead to a generalized state of ill health the end result of which could be cancer. In his opinion: 'Nutrition is the most important environmental factor within our control.' Finally Gerson[4] emphasized the role of poor nutrition as a major predisposing cause of cancer. He demonstrated also the beneficial effect of corrected nutrition, in treating cancer once it was established.

Nutrition is seen to be a major factor in producing a general decline in the individual's level of health. This allows the myriad toxic and irritant factors in the environment greater opportunity to act on one area or another of the body and to produce cancerous changes. Diet can by its influence on the chemistry of the body produce the devitalized and toxic state that many regard as the precursor of cancer.

Davidson, an orthodox scientist, Professor of Medicine at

Aberdeen and Edinburgh Universities, conjectures[5] that in theory it should be possible to devise a diet on which healthy tissues could survive and tumours cease to grow. The diet discussed herein together with a suitable intake of nitrilosides (Laetrile) could be the answer to his search.

Donald German M.D.,[6] Clinical Professor of Radiology at the University of Missouri School of Medicine, states unequivocally that diet is a major causative factor in at least 50 per cent of female cancers and more than a third of male cancers. He estimates that approximately 240,000 new cancer cases each year could be avoided in the U.S.A. alone, if the victims knew how to choose their food more sensibly. He further suggests that the average individual can reduce the risk of developing cancer by 80 per cent by simple dietary changes. Unfortunately, in my opinion, Dr German does not go far enough. Were he to advocate a diet rich in vitamin B_{17}, as well as the excellent pattern of eating (low fat, low animal protein, high vegetable) that he promotes, then a much better statistical projection could be forecast. It is interesting that although he does not mention vitamin B_{17}, Dr German advocates very strongly a number of the foods known to be rich in this substance such as spinach, sweet potatoes, lima beans and green peas.

Herberger[3] states categorically that cancer is almost unknown amongst people living on natural (i.e. unprocessed) food. We can certainly investigate this claim, insofar as it has been documented. What is even more interesting is to note that the healthiest of these primitive peoples are those amongst whom a diet rich in nitrilosides (B_{17}) is common.

In West Africa there are several well-authenticated reports of the absence of cancer amongst the native people, prior to a western dietary pattern being introduced. Professor Albert Schweitzer[7] stated that 'The seldom and infrequent occurrence of cancer in this country is connected with ... the diet. We did not have any cancer cases in our hospital.' The noted Japanese scientist George Ohsawa[8] commented on the high proportion of cassava eaten at Lambaréné and more recently Lawrence Knight F.R.C.S.[9] spent many months working in the hospitals of Sierra Leone. He states that he did not come across a single case of cancer.

As mentioned, the diet in this part of tropical Africa contains a large amount of cassava which is rich in nitrilosides (vitamin

B17). Cassava has a very low protein content and is high in carbohydrates. It is basically undesirable as a main source of food. Deficiency conditions can and do arise from its use in a subsistence economy. Despite this, amongst often poorly nourished tribesmen, cancer is almost unheard of.

In far more idyllic surroundings live the Hunza people of Northern India. Living as they do in isolated valley communities they have been a much investigated people. The main source of interest has been their extreme longevity and vitality into advanced age. Active individuals of well over a hundred years of age are common. From the viewpoint of our current interest it should be noted that cancer is unknown to the Hunzas. These people have been studied by doctors and scientists for over half a century. Sir Robert McCarrison found them to be largely vegetarians, long-lived, healthy and happy, He found no evidence of cancer. Their diet he stated, largely comprised fresh and dried apricots, of which they also ate the pits. They also ate fresh vegetables, buckwheat, millet, alfalfa and various beans. These foods all contain nitrilosides in large concentrations, the apricot pit being the main source. Unlike the tribesmen of Africa, whose protection against cancer derives from the intake of cassava, the Hunza people live on a more balanced diet and thus enjoy health as well as immunity to cancer.

Griffin[15] makes the important point that the Hunza people do not carry their immunity with them. Those of the valley people who have moved away and who have adopted the diets of their new country, have developed the diseases of those countries, including cancer.

Similar groups of people are to be found in the tropical rain forests of South America, the Abkhasian people of the Caucasus, the North American Indian (before a Western diet was adopted) and primitive people in the Pacific islands. The common factor among all of them is a diet relatively low in animal protein, low in carbohydrates, high in vegetable protein, minerals and vitamins and high in nitrilosides. We can also examine modified diets amongst certain groups living in civilized societies.

The Seventh-Day Adventists are a religious sect who avoid meat, tea, coffee and other stimulants, as part of their beliefs. Over 500,000 of these people live in America. In all other ways they are an integrated part of the community and can be statistically compared. They show an incidence of cancer which is less than 50 per cent of that of the total population. Now since these people do not drink alcohol, or smoke cigarettes it might be argued that this is the truly significant difference between the Seventh-Day Adventists and the rest of the population. Donald German M.D.[6] has researched this subject with great thoroughness and is adamant that the cancer rate amongst this group is 30 to 50 per cent lower than other groups who are non-smoking, non-drinking but not vegetarian.

As Griffin points out, many of these people become vegetarian late in life; some do not stick rigidly to the diet and those that do may not necessarily be replacing the animal protein with an adequate vegetable intake. For these reasons, and also as a result of most of their food being both chemically fertilized and sprayed, they do not enjoy quite the protection that the Hunza people do.

Phillips[10] has made a number of suggestions as to the dietary factors that influence the low cancer rate among Seventh-Day Adventists. He makes the point that just as test animals on a low fat and low protein diet develop fewer tumours than animals on an unrestricted diet, so might the low protein and fat intake of this sect be a major factor. The high intake of vitamins C and A in their diet is also believed to give protection against certain carcinogens.

A diet low in animal protein would appear to keep the body's immunization system (its defence mechanism) in a more actively alert state, enabling it to deal effectively with any early cancer development. A 50 per cent reduction in the incidence of cancer amongst Seventh-Day Adventists is a remarkable figure and must show what would be possible were government agencies and the medical profession to attempt to educate the population in the possible benefits of rational dietetics.

Similar evidence can be produced from populations 'deprived' of civilized foodstuffs by war time or famine conditions. During the Second World War many European people were forced to eat basic vegetable and brown bread diets with a reduced animal protein intake. Without exception, despite the stress of those times, the health of such populations improved and the incidence of cancer decreased — until, of course, normality returned and eating habits were re-established, and cancer once again became prevalent. Figures supporting these facts are available in Denmark, Holland and other European countries.

The Fat Connection

Dr Henry Bieler[11] believes that the high protein diet of the West may be responsible for the increase in cancer. If meat is to be eaten, he theorizes, it should be eaten raw or very lightly cooked. He stresses that he does not advocate meat eating but that clinical and experimental evidence is available to show that cooked meat is infinitely more toxic than fresh raw meat. Cooked meat is less digestible and more subject to putrefaction. Bieler has had success in treating many chronic diseases, including cancer, by diet alone — always, it should be stressed, a vegetarian diet.

Fat in the diet is another important consideration. Animal research at the Naylor Dana Institute for Disease Prevention[12] has shown that a high fat intake increases the risk of breast cancer. Cholesterol is a fat-like substance found in all animal protein foods. German has shown a highly significant connection between the development of cancer (especially of the colon) and the intake of dietary fat, particularly cholesterol.

It is worth emphasizing that a vegetarian diet alone does not guarantee protection from cancer. There are good and bad vegetarian diets. To stop eating animal products and continue eating refined, processed and generally devitalized food is no way to build a healthier body, or prevent cancer.

In considering diet in relation to the treatment of cancer there appears to be a great deal of evidence to support a *totally* vegetarian diet. Dr Max Gerson,[13] in evidence before a U.S. Senate committee, stated that cancer responded well to a diet consisting mainly of fresh fruit and vegetables and which excluded milk, meat, alcohol and processed foods. He said: 'We know that a healing aparatus is present and functions in a healthy body, and we have learned that by means of this treatment [i.e. dietary] that it can be reactivated if the body can be sufficiently detoxified in cancer.' The means he used to detoxify the body were through a vegetarian diet which excluded processed and devitalized foods and animal protein and salt. He stressed, as I shall, that during the detoxifying process the patient may well feel lethargic and unwell at times, as a result of the release into the bloodstream of toxic waste products with which the body's organs of elimination will be attempting to deal.

Gerson's diet, as stated, was limited to fruit and vegetables, grains and after a period of some months, yogurt and skimmed milk. His desire was to eliminate sodium from the tissues, to detoxify the body and to enrich it with potassium. He also included certain vitamins and enzymes. Dr Maud Fere,[14] who treated herself successfully for cancer, and subsequently treated many hundreds of cancer patients, insisted that the cancer patient should adopt a vegetarian diet and should keep strictly to it until they are absolutely cured — that is, when their vitality is fully restored, which may take up to two years of strict perseverance. She too forbade the use of salt and used a number of supplements (such as dilute hydrochloric acid).

Dr Kirstine Nolfi[13] also treated herself successfully, for cancer of the breast, with a completely raw (uncooked) vegetarian diet. She too treated many similar cases subsequently by these methods. Bircher-Benner treated all types of disease, including cancer, with the same basic approach — a corrected diet. He stated that 'The ideal equilibrium of all nutritional factors needed by the human organism is alone supplied by a mixed diet compiled of integrals of plant life, largely in its natural state. I say this with a full sense of responsibility as a medical man, not merely as an abstainer from flesh food.'

W. Kollath stated that cancer patients should have fresh fruit available all day, and that vegetables should figure prominently in their diets. He advised the use of onions and garlic, both rich in sulphur. The diet of the cancer patient, he felt, should also include unsaturated fatty acids such as are found in linseed, sunflower seeds, and wheatgerm. Vegetable oils were always to be preferred to animal fat. Herberger is in general agreement that animal protein should be restricted and that a basically raw vegetarian diet should be adopted by cancer patients.

Dr J. Issels, the famous German cancer specialist, places his patients on a fruit and vegetable diet before continuing with his 'combination therapy' which attempts to restore the body's ability to fight the disease itself. Dr William Kelley,[15] who has also treated himself successfully for cancer, places his patients on a vegetarian diet which excludes dairy products. He places great stress on the use of almonds and pancreatic enzymes, certain vitamins and the herb comfrey. Dr Kelley also recommends the use of diluted hydrochloric acid (in tablet form), as does Dr Fere, in order to assist the digestive process.

Dr H. Moolenburgh of Holland stresses that Laetrile, with which he treats his cancer patients, should be built into the whole therapeutic scheme:[16] 'I place them on a buttermilk, vegetarian raw food diet, megavitamins, minerals, enzymes and Laetrile.' Dr John Richardson one of America's leading advocates of Laetrile insists on a diet of fresh fruits, vegetables, seeds, nuts and grains. All animal protein including dairy products are forbidden. In his view cancer should be identified as a deficiency disease caused by a lack of vitamin B_{17} and pancreatic enzymes or both. After using Laetrile for some time Richardson introduced a vegetarian diet: 'For the first time in my entire medical career, I began to see "terminal" cancer patients return to normal lives of health and vigour.' The well documented cases quoted in detail in Dr Richardson's book should be read by all those interested in the treatment of cancer.

These methods all vary in emphasis. Some stress the use of supplements not advocated by others. In some of their methods they even contradict each other. However, on the fundamental importance of a vegetarian diet, they all agree.

No single factor is more important to the cancer patient than diet. Whatever additional help the body receives from enzymes, minerals and vitamins, although vitally important, the basic day-to-day habits of eating will largely determine the degree and rate of potential recovery.

In the next chapter the diet relating to the treatment of patients with cancer will be presented. In a later chapter we will discuss a recommended diet that achieves the maximum intake of vitamin B_{17} and so helps to build a resistance to the onset of a cancerous condition. It should not be thought, however, that simply eating foods rich in B_{17} will give the individual immunity and the licence to break all the other rules of sound nutrition. We live in a world where the quality of all that we consume is tainted by chemical and other pollutants. With the greatest care it is yet difficult to ensure a whole and nutritious diet under 'civilized' conditions.

But by using the knowledge of those foods which offer us extra protection against disease we add to our chance of healthy living, though it is still up to each individual to decide to what extent responsibility for health will be accepted. Happiness is the ambition of all men and women; without health, I believe, there can be only a qualified and diminished degree of happiness. The quality of life stems from the extent to which we heed the laws that govern our existence. We can certainly break the rules, but just as certainly we must pay the price. The laws of diet and nutrition are becoming more clear. If they are rejected as being 'too difficult' or 'impractical', then at the very least the individual can never again claim ignorance or innocence. The rules are clear; the consequences too, are unmistakable.

[1] M. Bircher-Benner, *The Hell of Ill Health*, John Miles Publishers, 1940.

[2] F. Hoffman, *Cancer and Diet*, Williams and Wilkins, Baltimore, 1937.

[3] W. Herberger, *The Treatment of Inoperable Cancer*, John Wright and Son, 1965.

[4] Max Gerson, *A Cancer Therapy*, Dura Books, 1958.

[5] Sir Stanley Davidson, R. Passmore, J.F. Brock and A. Truswell, *Human Nutrition and Dietetics*, 6th edition, Churchill Livingstone, 1975.

[6] D. German, *The Anti-Cancer Diet*, Wydon Books, 1978.

[7] A. Schweitzer, *Letters from Lambaréné Hospital*, 1954.

[8] G. Ohsawa, *Cancer and the Philosphy of the Far East*, Ohsawa Foundation, 1964.

[9] Boris Chaitow, *A Timely Warning to a Sick Society*, published by the author, 1977.

[10] R.L. Phillips, 'Role of Life-Style and Dietary Habits in Risk of Cancer among Seventh-Day Adventists', *Cancer Research*, 35.

[11] H. Bieler, *Food is Your Best Medicine*, Neville Spearman, 1968.

[12] Po-Chuan and Cohen, 'Dietary Fat and Growth Promotion of Rat Mammary Tumours', *Cancer Research*, 35.

[13] C. Frazer MacKenzie, *Your Life is At Stake*.

[14] M. Fere, *Does Diet Cure Cancer?*, Thorsons, 1971.

[15] W. Kelley, *One Answer to Cancer*, Kelley Foundation, 1974.

[16] Personal communication to the author, 1977.

4

Diet for Cancer Patients

Before considering the recommended diet it will be as well to spend a little time dealing with those foods which the patient is going to eliminate from the diet. There are several factors that are vitally important to the cancer patient. First, in my opinion, is to ensure that nothing is taken into the body (or done to the body) that has harmful side effects, such as an increase in toxicity. It is also highly desirable that the body should be given every opportunity to eliminate toxic accumulations that have built up over the years. For a number of reasons animal protein foods (meat, fish, eggs, cheese and milk) are considered to add to the toxic load already present in the body. This is the opinion of numerous experts, previously quoted, such as Bircher-Benner, Issels, Richardson, Moolenburgh, Kelley and Gerson.

Meat and fish contain various toxic breakdown products that require extra efforts on the part of the body. In a state of chronic ill-health it would be unable to make such an effort. This may lead to only partial digestion of food, which would then undergo putrefaction. The organs of detoxification, such as the liver, already struggling to cope with the demands of a sick body, could not detoxify such additional poisons.

Thus, not only does such food fail to nourish but it also adds to the toxic state of the system by the addition of metabolic waste products. Also, by demanding the utilization of proteolytic enzymes for their digestion, such foods divert these cancer-destroying enzymes from that task. Remember that these enzymes act on the protein coat of the cancer cells, allowing the white blood cells to attack and destroy them.

Major research on this subject has been carried out by the Nobel prize winner Francois Jacob of the Pasteur Institute. He calls this process 'enzymatic de-shielding'. He points out that the protein mucus, the coat which is formed round cancer cells, deactivates and screens off from the cancer cells the body's 'soldiers', the leukocytes and the macrophages. It is therefore vital that the enzymes, which are able to remove this protective shield, be left to get on with their job rather than being diverted to digesting meat or fish. A further important consideration is that much meat contains oestrogen, with which many farmers 'improve' their animals prior to slaughter. Since this hormone is a prime cause of cancer it must on no account be included in the patient's diet. Dr Nieper[1] quotes the case of a colleague, suffering from lung cancer, who demonstrated the degree of stimulation to cancer tissue that eating chicken reared by the battery method produced. Most commercial beef and fowl producers utilize hormones in their animal feed.

The intake of eggs, butter, cheese and milk should be stopped, at least in the early stages of treatment. It might be that a little goat's milk yogurt or sour milk would be allowable, but the same fundamental objections that apply to meat and fish also apply to most dairy products. Milk contains hormones, a result of the prime purpose of milk, which is to provide stimulating food for the growth of the young animal. In order to digest cow's milk the human digestive system is called upon to perform feats for which it was not designed. Goat's milk is much better tolerated because of its different fat content but it still employs the protein digesting enzymes in its breakdown.

Natural unpasteurized goat's milk yogurt provides a virtually pre-digested food, rich in helpful bacteria, for the digestive system. It is therefore reasonable to include this in moderate quantities in the patient's diet.

Cheese is an extremely concentrated protein and usually contains salt, which is forbidden to the cancer patient, and is therefore unacceptable in the diet. A number of authorities (for instance, Herberger and Kelley) suggest that egg yolks are a desirable source of the amino-acids required by the body. My own view is that like all other animal proteins they should not be included in the diet. Amino-acids are available, through the judicious mixture of cereals and pulses, in a far more acceptable form.

Wynne-Tyson[2] points out graphically 'regardless of the known cancer-producing substances that are injected into animals in the pursuit of greater profit and in the hope of combating the ever more threatening diseases that factory farming, and other unnatural methods of stock care bring about, suspicion has been directed at meat itself as a contributory or even causative source of cancer'. He goes on, 'Decomposition begins as soon as an animal is slaughtered. Its blood stream, just like our own, serves as a debris conveyor for toxic wastes... To give our system the additional job of eliminating another creature's unwanted material together with the toxins of fear that are released into its bloodstream prior to slaughter seems to suggest, at the least, a very unaesthetic regard for the joys of nutrition.'

The omission from the diet of all animal proteins (barring natural, unpasteurized goat's milk yogurt) is the most important single dietary step that the cancer patient will have to take. Items thus eliminated are easily and acceptably replaced.

If we are to ensure that foods and beverages consumed are both nutritious and non-toxic, then the diet should contain no salt. As has been pointed out a number of cancer experts have condemned salt, in all its forms, as being an irritant. Some, such as Seeger, Gerson and Fere, believe that it stimulates cancer formation. It is also, of course, necessary to eliminate bicarbonate of soda (baking soda) in both cooking and as a digestive aid in various 'health' salts. Joosens[3] in 1973 showed that stomach cancer correlates with high salt intake.

All foods containing artificial colouring or preservatives are unacceptable in the patient's diet. This will mean that all preserves, pickles, jams, smoked, packaged or tinned foods, should not be eaten. It is also advisable to eliminate the use of toxic stimulants such as coffee, tea, alcohol, cocoa and chocolate. There are numerous beverages which are both pleasant and acceptable and these will be listed later in this chapter.

The diet must, as far as possible, exclude all refined products. Thus all white flour products and all sugar based products must be replaced with wholemeal cereal products and natural sweeteners such as honey or maple syrup. It should not be necessary to stress that tobacco usage should be stopped.

The following summarizes those foods and 'non-foods' which are prohibited, at least for the first twelve months of treatment of the cancer patient, who should also be using vitamin, mineral and enzyme supplementation, including Laetrile.

Prohibited foods

Meat	Eggs
Meat extracts	Cheese
Meat gravies and stock cubes	Margarine
Poultry	Butter
Fish	Milk
Shell fish	Ice Cream
Fish paste	Salt
Pepper	Cane or Beet sugar products
Curry	Preserves (jam,etc)
Ketchup	Tinned fruit
Pickles	Olives (green or black)
Mustard	Sulphur-dried fruit
Chillies	Frozen vegetables/fruit
Vinegar	Tinned vegetables/fruit
Tea	Salted or roasted nuts
Coffee	Tinned or packet soups
Alcohol	Anything containing
Soft drinks	preservatives, colouring or
White rice	chemical additives
All processed cereals	Saturated oils and fats
(puffed, flaked, etc)	Fried food
Pasta (macaroni, spaghetti,	Roasted food
noodles)	Fluoridated water

Hygienic considerations

The cancer patient should avoid remaining in a room where tobacco is being smoked. All synthetic cosmetics, anti-perspirants, toxic hairsprays, coal tar derived lipsticks,[4] and so on, should be avoided. Natural cosmetics are available at most health food stores.

Foods to be taken in very limited quantities

Mushrooms	Cashew nuts
Vichy water (high in salt)	Peanuts
Citrus fruit	Cucumber
Natural goat's milk yogurt	Celery

Foods that should be eaten
All vegetables including as many of the following as possible:

Alfalfa*	Comfrey
Artichokes (globe and	Chives
Jerusalem)	Cassava*
Asparagus	Chinese leaves
Aubergine	Dandelion
Brussel sprouts	French beans
Beets	Garlic
Beet top*	Kale
Cabbage	Leek
Carrots	Lettuce
Cauliflower	Okra (ladies' fingers)
Chicory	Seaweed
Onions	Spinach*
Parsley	Sweet potatoes*
Parsnips	Tomatoes
Peppers (green)	Turnips
Potatoes	Watercress*
Pumpkin	Yams*
Runner beans	
Radish	

*Items thus marked contain vitamin B_{17}

Wherever possible vegetables should be organically grown (that is, free of chemical fertilizers and sprays). It is now increasingly possible to find suppliers of such produce in most areas. A number of organizations exist to promote organic farming and reference to these will be found in the General Information section (page 153). Home grown vegetables should also be produced without artificial fertilizers or sprays. Advice is available from books, health magazines, gardening magazines and various organizations.

The reason for urging the consumption of organically produced vegetables as opposed to those commercially produced, lies in their relative value as nutrients. Since the introduction of chemical fertilizers in vegetable production the vitamin and mineral content has diminished markedly. Vegetables can only take from the soil the substances it contains. The result of applying chemicals such as nitrogen, phosphorus and potassium, in their inorganic forms, to the soil is to produce crops that grow quickly and look attractive, but which are deficient in a number of vital factors which, as a result, are low in disease resistance and offer poor food value. Since it is the aim of this diet to rebuild health through sound nutrition, it is as well to start from the very foundation of nutrition, the soil.

Vegetables should be consumed in as fresh a state as possible. The reason, again, is the self-evident one of retaining vitamin and mineral content. For this reason cooking should be kept to a minimum. Light steaming of vegetables is all the cooking that should be necessary. In order to derive the most nutritional value from vegetables they should be eaten raw, as mixed salads. Remember that the skins of many vegetables contain the greatest concentration of minerals and should therefore not be discarded.

The golden rules are:
1. Eat organically grown, unsprayed vegetables, wherever possible.
2. Eat them as fresh as possible.
3. Avoid frozen, salted and tinned vegetables.
4. Avoid soaking or overcooking vegetables, so that vitamins and minerals are retained.
5. Avoid peeling vegetables for the same reason.
6. Raw food is almost always more nutritous than cooked. (An exception are carrots where light cooking makes pro-vitamin A more easily acceptable for digestion.)

Sprouted Seeds, Grains and Beans

Alfalfa*	Lentils*
Aduki beans	Sunflower seeds
Chickpeas*(Garbanzo)	Corn
Soya Beans	Barley
Mung beans*	Oats
Wheat	Fenugreek
Buckwheat*	Rye

*Contain vitamin B_{17}

There are many other beans and seeds that may be successfully sprouted. It is important to remember that seeds of potato and tomato, if sprouted, are poisonous.

The nutritive value of sprouted seeds and beans would be difficult to exaggerate. They are easy to digest, as a result of the chemical changes within the growing sprouts, which alters the carbohydrate and protein structure of the seed. The vitamin content is high in sprouts because of the dramatic process of growth. This includes vitamins A, B_2, B_6, C, E and K. Various minerals such as iron, magnesium and calcium are also present in easily digested forms. In addition to all these valuable attributes, sprouts are delicious to eat.

Many books are available in Health Stores giving details of sprouting techniques. It will be found to be extremely simple and most rewarding. Sprouts can be added to salads or used as sandwich fillers.

Cereals

Barley	Oats
Bran	Rice
Buckwheat*	Rye
Corn	Wheat
Millet*	

*Contain vitamin B_{17}

Cereals should always be whole and unprocessed. Health Stores and many grocery chains now supply unpolished rice and wholemeal flour. Cereals in combination with pulses (beans, peas and lentils, etc.) in such dishes as soups or stews will provide the body with all the essential amino-acids. This means that the body is not being deprived of 'first-class' protein because of the exclusion of flesh foods.

Pulses

Blackeye beans*	Lentils*
Butter beans	Lima beans*
Chickpeas*	Mung beans*
Green peas*	Soya beans
Kidney beans*	

*Contain vitamin B_{17}

These nutritious and delicious foods provide the possibility of interesting variations in the diet. Remember that foods from this group should be combined with a cereal, such as unpolished rice, in order to make up complete protein nourishment.

Nuts

Almond*	Pecan
Cashew*	Walnut
Filbert	Hazelnut
Macadamia*	

*Contain vitamin B$_{17}$

These foods are packed with vitamins, minerals and good quality protein. Cashews and Brazils have a fairly high fat content and so should be used sparingly. Almonds are particularly valuable to the diet. It is desirable to shell your own nuts as there is a considerable loss of vitamin B once they have been removed from the shell. Commercial packing of nuts can lead to the oils becoming rancid and it is possible that packaged nuts will have been chemically treated to slow down this process. On no account should roasted or salted nuts be eaten.

There is some controversy surrounding the use of peanuts (which are not nuts but beans) and for the purpose of this diet they should be excluded or used very sparingly.

Seeds

Apple*	Cherry*
Sesame	Pear*
Pumpkin	Peach*
Sunflower	Plum or Prune*
Linseed*	Nectarine*
Apricot*	

*Contain vitamin B$_{17}$

Pumpkin and sunflower seeds can be eaten as a snack, with cereals or on salads. Linseed can be sprinkled on soup or salads or mixed with cereals. The pits of the various fruits can be ground and sprinkled on salads, soups or cereals. Apple and pear pips should be eaten with the fruit. *Patients taking Laetrile should avoid concentrated quantities of B$_{17}$ rich foods at the same time that Laetrile is taken.* These foods combine well with cereals and pulses to provide all the essential amino-acids.

Fresh Fruits

Apples
Apricots
Avocado pears
Bananas
Blackberries*
Boysenberries*
Cherries
Cranberries*
Currants (red & black)*
Elderberries*
Figs
Gooseberries*
Grapes
Guavas*
Huckleberries*

Litchies
Mulberries*
Mangoes
Melons
Nectarines
Papayas
Pears
Peaches
Pineapples
Plums
Quinces
Raspberries*
Strawberries*
Watermelons

*Contain vitamin B_{17}

These cleansing, nutritious foods are intended to play a major part in the patient's detoxification programme. A completely satisfying and nourishing meal can be built around fruit. It is suggested that at least one of the day's meals should comprise mainly fruit. Suggestions will be given as to how to balance the diet later in this chapter. Citrus fruit is not recommended in the early stages of the diet (first six to twelve months).

Dried Fruit

Apple rings
Apricots
Figs
Pears

Peaches
Prunes
Raisins
Currants*

*Contain vitamin B_{17}

These fruits must only be eaten if sun-dried. Sulphur or other chemical drying methods are not desirable. After washing, these fruits can be eaten alone or mixed with fresh fruit or cereals. Lightly cooked, or soaked to soften them, they are nutritious and tasty.

Juices

All the vegetables and fruits mentioned can be juiced. Mixtures such as carrots and apple are especially beneficial. This method of obtaining nutrients must be used sparingly, however, as there is often a tendency to drink large quantities of unmasticated vegetable and fruit in this manner. This can lead to indigestion since the process of carbohydrate digestion begins in the mouth and depends on food being adequately mixed with saliva prior to swallowing. Juices therefore may be taken as an aperitif and each mouthful should be retained until it has been mixed well with saliva.

It is also important for the digestive system to have an adequate fibre intake. The juicing process removes all of the roughage from food. Bowel function should be assisted by adding fibre such as unprocessed bran to the diet and by keeping the consumption of juices to moderate levels.

Beverages

Herb Tea

Alfalfa

Comfrey

Camomile

Linseed

Linden blossom (lime)

Rosehip

Red sage

Red Clover

Sage

Peppermint

Rooibosch and many more

Coffee substitute

Caro

Dandelion Coffee

Pioneer

Swiss Cup

Other drinks

Nut or Soya milk

Bottled Spa water, not if of a high bicarbonate of soda ($NaHCO_3$) or salt ($NaCl$) content (such as Vichy water).

Avoid tap-water, especially if fluoridated. Individual tastes vary and what is palatable to one is not necessarily so to another. Experimentation with the subtle flavours of the various herb teas will lead to eventual satisfaction. If sweeteners are found to be necessary they should be used sparingly and may be chosen from the following:

Honey
Date Sugar
Maple Syrup

Flavouring Cooking

Chives	Sage
Garlic	Thyme and other savoury herbs
Onion	Kelp
Oregano	Vegetable seasoning (free of salt)
Parsley	'Ruthmol' (potassium chloride) salt substitute

The art of seasoning and flavouring foods with natural herbs should be acquired. Reference to the books listed in the appendix will assist those not familiar with these subtle aids to cooking.

Oils and Fats

Olive oil	Soya oil
Safflower oil	Nut spreads
Sunflower oil	Soya Lecithin spread
Sesame oil	Avocado spread

Dressing a salad with oil and a sprinkling of a herb, such as oregano, or crushing a little garlic over a salad will add to the enjoyment by enhancing the flavours. Oils should be cold pressed if possible.

Lactic Acid Foods

J. Kuhl has demonstrated the value to the cancer patient of foods containing lactic acid. These include *sauerkraut*, beans and gherkins which have been prepared with lactic acid. These are obtainable from most health food stores. *Ensure that such preparations are in fact made with lactic acid.*

Additional Foods

Buckwheat noodles	Miso (fermented soya beans)
Buckwheat macaroni	Tahini (sesame paste)
Soya flour dishes	Hummus (chickpea paste)
Wholemeal pasta	Seaweed (Hidziki, Agar-Agar, etc)

With the addition of these foods to the foregoing lists the diet available will be seen to be potentially exciting and varied. Rather than feeling that there is deprivation and an enforced 'giving up' of habitually eaten foods, the individual would do well to embark on the adventure of the new way of eating with an enquiring and positive approach. Half the world's population live on just such a diet and let it be never forgotten that they seldom, if ever, contract degenerative diseases, including cancer, until they begin to adopt a Western 'civilized' diet.

The variety of foods available on this diet make it necessary to guide the patient as to the most desirable pattern to adopt. Making allowances for particular personal factors, the following would be the ideal routine to follow:

Breakfast
Choose from:
Fresh fruit
Soaked dried fruit
Muesli — cereal/nut/seed mixture moistened with fruit juice or nutmilk or yogurt (see recipe)
Nuts
Wholemeal toast and lecithin spread
Herb tea or coffee substitute

This meal should be taken at approximately 8 a.m. The various supplements that should accompany the various meals will be explained in a later chapter.

Midday Meal
Choose from:
Mixed raw salad
Nuts, seeds, sprouted seeds and beans
Oil dressing
Baked jacket potato and nut butter *or*
Wholemeal bread and nut butter or spread *or*
Vegetable/Lentil/Rice/Cereal/Bean Dish
Wholemeal or Rye bread

Dessert
Fresh fruit and nuts and sprouts

This meal should be eaten approximately four hours after breakfast.

Mid-afternoon
Herb tea or fruit or vegetable drink
If hungry, fresh fruit, seeds and nuts may be eaten.

Evening Meal
If no salad was eaten at the midday meal then it should be the major part of the evening meal. If a salad was eaten at the midday meal then the evening meal should consist primarily of a savoury dish made from beans, cereals, vegetables, etc. If possible include a side salad and always finish with fruit (fresh or lightly cooked) and nuts.

This meal should be eaten at 6 to 7 p.m. unless a reasonably large fruit and seed meal was eaten in the mid-afternoon in which case the evening meal could be set back to 8 p.m. or so. The reason for this pattern of eating is that a number of supplements are taken at the same time as food and the timing of these is of some importance.

Potassium Broth
Nourishing drinks can be made in the following way.

Wash and chop four large carrots, a few sprays of parsley, six spinach leaves, and any two of the following: asparagus, potato skin, lettuce leaves, beet tops, onion, turnip tops. One celery stalk may also be added.

Altogether four cupsful of chopped vegetables should be added to one and a half quarts of water in a stainless steel utensil. Cook slowly for 30 minutes. Strain and drink when warm. Any surplus may be refrigerated and used the next day, after warming.

If constipation is a problem a tablespoonful of flaxseed and a tablespoonful of bran can be soaked overnight in the broth. In the morning this should be warmed and drunk. It is not advisable to chew the seeds.[5]

Do not use seasoning containing sodium chloride (common or sea salt).

Salads
These should comprise as wide an assortment of the indicated vegetables, sprouting seeds and beans as possible. Root

vegetables may be finely grated and leafy vegetables shredded and mixed together just prior to eating. To this add seeds, sprouts and nuts. Eaten with a jacket potato or wholemeal bread and nut butter, the meal should be appetizing and delicious. Use a little crushed garlic or chopped onion and a recommended oil with lemon juice or apple cider vinegar as a dressing.

Food should be eaten slowly and chewed well. It is not desirable to drink with meals, apart from the limited quantity of liquid required to assist the swallowing of the various supplements. It is important for the patient to eat regularly and not to be tempted into skipping meals. The whole aim of the diet is to detoxify the body and to rebuild its vitality and so allow the defence mechanism to begin to operate against the disease.

Periodically, at least twice weekly, it would be advantageous to have a day on uncooked food only. As the patient gets to enjoy the fresh wholesome flavours of the various foods so will this seem less of a hardship. On such days the pattern of eating will be the same: only the content will vary. A second salad could be eaten in the evening or one of the main meals could be centred around fruit, for instance, avocado, apple, pear, banana, nuts and seeds. Such a meal is surprisingly filling and satisfying.

If thirsty, drink a small glass of fresh fruit or vegetable juice. Tap water should be avoided, especially if fluoridated. Bottled spring water may be used for herb tea preparation and cooking. Remember never to overcook food. The least possible exposure to heat, commensurate with edibility, is the target. If it is possible, aluminium cooking utensils should not be used (see Chapter 5 for suggested recipes).

After a period of enthusiasm, patients (especially if they are feeling stronger and less ill) may be tempted to include some of the 'forbidden' foods. The theory seems to be that a 'little of what you fancy' cannot hurt. Let it be very clear from the outset that the object of the treatment programme is to save life. The bedrock on which the various therapeutic methods are based is the diet of the patient. If a little bit of this, and a little bit of that (all contra-indicated, of course) are added to the diet, be certain that harm is being done and that a little will soon become a lot.

Friends, relatives and medical advisers will proffer advice. This may contradict the suggestion offered by this book. It would be well for the prospective patient to consider the arguments and theories expounded herein before electing to follow the methods that stem from these theories. In this way a firm resolve to see the programme through will result, and comments such as 'cancer is not going to be affected by what you eat' will not upset the patient's determination.

How long should the patient continue on this diet and with the supplements? The pattern of eating can be changed as progress becomes more established. If the patient is showing no signs of active disease and has gained weight, increased vitality and appetite and has an improved sense of well-being, a number of modifications to the diet would be in order.

The following might be added to the menu by degrees: two or three eggs weekly; a little butter may be used and goat's milk or skimmed milk, in moderation. If after eighteen months to two years the progress continues, as evidenced by more energy, weight gain, good appetite and no evidence of an active disease process, then fish may also be added to the menu once or twice weekly.

The supplements will also be modified and reduced. A constant maintenance dose of one gram of Laetrile daily is recommended. The general condition of the patient will determine other changes, apart from which the patient should regard the pattern of eating and supplementation as permanent.

Perhaps the situation faced by a diabetic patient could be used as an example. The diabetic may control his condition with insulin (by injection or orally) and a strict diet. Were such a patient to ignore the need to restrict the intake of sugar then catastrophic results would follow, even if the condition has been stable for years. In just such a way the cancer patient should maintain the programme as described.

[1] H. Nieper, 'Changes and Prospects in Medical Treatment of Cancer', *Medizin*, 1976.
[2] J. Wynne-Tyson, *Food for a Future*, Centaur, 1976.
[3] Sir Stanley Davidson, R. Passmore, J.F. Brock and A. Trusswell, *Human Nutrition and Dietetics*, 6th edition, Churchill Livingstone, 1975.
[4] *Physicians Handbook of Vitamin B₁₇ Therapy*, McNaughton Foundation, 1975.
[5] Paavo Aivola, *Health Secrets from Europe*, Arco, 1975.

5

Preventing Cancer

In considering those aspects of our daily life which we can alter, modify or control, in order to enhance our chances of avoiding cancer, nutrition is the factor deserving of our greatest attention. For the majority of people there is the possibility of change if they wish.

In 1976 Dr G. Gori, Deputy Director of the National Cancer Institute's division of Cancer Cause and Prevention, told a Senate Select Committee that improper diet is directly related to 60 per cent of all types of cancer in women and 40 per cent in men. This is probably a wildly inaccurate understatement, but coming as it does from the very heart of orthodox conservatism it should be seen as profoundly significant.

The first barrier to cross is that of ignorance of the facts. If we do not know of the connection between what we eat and our state of health then we are unlikely to be aware of the link between diet and cancer. Our first task is to examine what evidence there is to support this connection, and to so satisfy ourselves of its absolute and demonstrable validity.

There is no shadow of doubt as to the relationship between smoking and cancer, although, as mentioned in Chapter 1, this is not a clear case of cause and effect, since nine out of ten smokers fail to develop cancer. No doubt some of the nine die of other smoking-related diseases, such as coronary disease, before cancer has time to become manifest. Nevertheless, smoking, whilst a major element in some cancers, is not the underlying cause — this lies in the biochemical and psychological state of the smoker. The prospect of cancer developing is patently increased by the nicotine habit and yet this knowledge does not deter the majority of smokers. Knowledge alone is not enough, it must be accompanied by motivation. There is a strange reluctance in many people to recognize the obvious dangers inherent in so many unhealthy habits.

One reason for this is the failure to distinguish between health, as indicated by the absence of obvious signs of disease, and health, as indicated by a state of positive well-being. In everyday life, where the norm is a state of second class health, it is an accepted part of life for the majority of people to suffer from minor symptoms such as headaches, indigestion, constipation, insomnia, irritability and depression, skin problems, stiffness, aches and pains, etc., etc., it is perhaps understandable that inertia exists towards major changes in the lifestyle. If these, and other, symptoms are almost universally 'enjoyed', then one argument suggests that it must indeed be 'normal' and natural. None of these symptoms, after all, threatens life itself. However, where our very existence is concerned, surely motivation should be forthcoming to deal with the threat? For those who care, and want to live for the sake of living, there is much that can be done. There are a number of outward signs and symptoms which can indicate early evidence of a pre-cancerous condition. Many of these are simple vitamin deficiency signs, and the presence of several of them should cause no alarm. *It does not mean that cancer is lurking or inevitable.* However, all these signs are undesirable and most are reversible with very little effort. Should more than six or seven of these signs be present it would be as well to take professional advice and to concentrate of the dietetic and other advice given in this chapter.

Signs to watch for, indicating a state of ill-health which could, together, with other factors, lead to cancer, include:

Skin: Changes in texture such as dryness and a tendency to crack. Flaking, especially on the thighs and lower abdomen. Yellow/grey pallor.

Tongue and Inner Lips: These may be bright red ('like horsemeat' says Dr Moolenburgh).

Corners of Mouth: These may develop cracks.

Gums: These may recede and bleed easily after brushing or eating.

Corners of Nose: May develop scaling and become reddened.

Nails: May be brittle; or ridged. They may contain white flecks.

Hair: This may become lifeless and thin with a tendency to scurf.

Lower legs: These may develop oedema (puffy swelling) especially on the inner aspects, which are often very sensitive to pressure.

Bruising: This may occur more easily than is warranted.

A general decline in vitality may take place, as evidenced by apathy and listlessness.

Cuts and Grazes: These may be slow to heal and show a tendency to sepsis.

Appetite: This may be poor, accompanied by a general loss of weight.

Unnatural Tiredness: This, as well as lack of energy after sleep, may be felt. Blood tests may indicate a degree of iron deficiency anaemia and an increase in erythrocyte sedimentation rate.

Moolenburgh describes the cancer-prone individual as having been 'buffeted by fate'. A series of personal shocks and emotional disasters having been endured, these individuals are often characterized by a resigned state of submission, a silent depression. There is frequently a deficiency of faith. Moolenburgh points out that cancer patients frequently have no spiritual convictions at all. Statistically the difference between cancer sufferers and the general population in this regard is significant. Moolenburgh frequently asks his patients such questions as: 'When did you last see an angel?' more to assess the nature of their response than in the hope of a positive sighting. However, he reports that some individuals do display a strong spiritual side and that these often make better progress than those who do not have any faith or spirituality.

A factor to be considered is the relevance of any close family history of cancer. When taken along with the general state of health, as evidenced by the type of indications mentioned above, a family history of malignant disease becomes significant.

The signs mentioned have been compiled by many practitioners including Drs Moerman, Kelley and Moolenburgh, and most of the signs involve, to some extent, the nutritional status of the individual.

It is important, before considering diet and supplements in any depth, to make it absolutely clear that there is no single programme which is right for everyone, either to retain or to regain health, or to prevent cancer. There are rules which apply to everyone but a key fact of life is summed up by the phrase 'biological individuality'. Simply explained this means that there exist different requirements for essential nutrients from one person to another, sometimes to a staggering degree. Unless we realize this, and attempt to modify the general rules to fit the particular needs of the individual, we will not be able to achieve an optimum level of health, or ensure adequate protection against degenerative diseases, including cancer. Linus Pauling[1], for example, points out that whilst some individuals can function at an optimum level of health on an intake of only a quarter of a gram of vitamin C daily, others require as much as 10 grams to remain in good health (i.e. symptom free and feeling positively well). This difference in needs has genetic origins, and the great research scientist who first propounded the theory of biochemical individuality, Dr Roger Williams, subtitled his book of that name '*The Basis for the Genetotrophic Concept*'. This concept can best be summed up in these words from the book: 'Individuality in nutritional needs is the basis for the genetotrophic approach and for the belief that nutrition applied with due concern for individual genetic variations, which may be large, offers the solution to many baffling health problems. This certainly is close to the heart of applied biochemistry.'

In practice this results in our having to, through a process which involves trial and error, define each individual's own needs for particular nutrients. It is not valid, or scientific, to say, for example, that we all need 1, 2 or 10 grams of vitamin C (or anything else) in order to regain, or to retain, health. It may be that on average a particular amount of a substance can be shown to be needed to prevent obvious deficiency symptoms from appearing, but this is only an average, around which there will occur great variations in terms of individual needs.

Research[2,3] has clearly demonstrated a further important consideration in our aim of preventing cancer. This is that in Western industrialized countries the majority of people suffer from a degree of sub-clinical nutrient deficiency. Indeed, it can be questioned whether it is possible for the majority of people, in such societies, to obtain adequate, never mind optimum, health and an adequate nutritional status, via food alone. This is due to a variety of factors including soil deficiencies, commercial practices in the production, marketing and preparation of foods, as well as the frankly inadequate dietary patterns of many people. Even if a reasonable dietary pattern exists it is debatable whether the food eaten actually contains a balanced compliment of essential nutrients. Supplementation is considered by many researchers to be a necessary adjunct to the eating of a wholefood dietary pattern in order to ensure that adequate nutrients actually reach the body.

Whether the individual is then able to digest, absorb and utilize the nutrients is another question. There is much evidence to suggest that inadequate digestive function (e.g. hydrochloric acid or pancreatic enzyme deficiency) is a key reason for a degree of relative malnutrition in many people.[4] Other factors including emotional stress, exercise levels being inadequate, environmental pollution, etc. are all involved in the creation of such states, as well as the previously discussed dietary patterns, inherited tendencies, and past illnesses. At any given time the individual's predisposition towards health or ill health (the current health status) is the culmination of all that he has inherited and all that has happened to him up to that point. The degree of resistance that he can display at any given time to any stress or insult is unique to himself. Disease, therefore, is to be seen as being multi-causal. There are few conditions, and cancer is certainly not one of them, in which there is a simple cause and effect picture. There are equally few 'magic bullets' in the treatment of ills which actually deal with the real causes of disease. Long-term development of problems of health require long-term solutions. This is why the individualization of therapy is vital.

Whilst having laboured the need for individualized nutritional patterns it is still possible to give general indications of what relationship has been established between particular nutrients and cancer prevention. The following is not totally comprehensive but it does give information on many aspects of this vital subject.

Vitamin A
Numerous studies[5] over a 20 year period show that carotene (which the body converts into vitamin A) significantly lowers the incidence of lung cancer, even in long-term smokers. The study appears to show that the source of vitamin A which offers the protection is not the ready-made animal source called retinol, but the vegetable β-carotene source. β-Carotene is also called pro-vitamin A since the body splits this to form vitamin A. Carrots, dark green leafy vegetables, green beans, some fruits, such as apricots, cantaloupe melons, persimmons, etc., are good sources of β-carotene[6,7].

Studies indicate that lowered carotene intake occurs before the development of cancer and not as a result of it. Recommendations for the use of additional supplementation of vitamin A vary, but the authoritative researcher Dr Carl Pfeiffer, of the Brain Bio Centre, and E.R. Bannerman, of the New York University School of Medicine,[8] suggest 50,000 IU daily. It has been established[9] that emulsified (water miscible) vitamin A is more readily absorbed by the body than the oil soluble form. Emulsified vitamin A is available in the U.K. from Cantassium Co. (See Appendix for address).

The B Vitamins
In terms of the prevention of cancer a number of the B vitamins have been found to be important. Hoffer and Walker[10], for example, point out that pyridoxene (vitamin B_6) deficiency predisposes towards cancer (together with zinc–see below). If any of the B vitamins are taken then all the others should be taken in a balanced combination. For example, to avoid an imbalance, the dosages of vitamin B_1, B_2 and B_6 should be the same[11]. If any of the other B vitamins are taken then B-complex should also be taken. To enhance B-complex effectiveness vitamin's C and E, calcium, chromium and phosphorus are also indicated. These, too, are listed by various authorities as playing a protective role against cancer.

Minerals
Whilst specific nutrients such as vitamin A have been shown to have a protective role in certain forms of cancer, in a more general sense the dependence of the body's immune system on adequate general nutrition, as well as on specific trace elements, deserves re-emphasis. Such substances as selenium, manganese, zinc and molybdenum, all offer protection against cancer as shown by a variety of research workers.[12] Selenium deficiency has been found to correlate with an increased susceptibility to cancer. It is associated with pancreatic insufficiency which has the effect of limiting the anti-tumour cell effect of proteolytic enzymes normally produced by the pancreas. Selenium also activates, and enhances, vitamin E in its role as a protector against oxidation-induced cellular damage.

Zinc levels have been found to be lowered in childhood leukaemia. Molybdenum deficiency is thought to be one of the key factors in the causation of oesophageal cancer.

Manganese is thought to activate the enzyme superoxide dismutase which prevents the accumulation of cancer forming mutagenic superoxide-anions. There are numerous other examples of the interrelationship between specific nutrients and the body's defence systems, including vitamins C and E. Recent reports from Japan[13] indicate that the trace element germanium has both a preventive and a therapeutic role in relation to cancer. One of the best sources of germanium is garlic (which is also rich in selenium). Reports from South Africa[14] have shown exciting anti-tumour effects from a completely non-toxic source. This is gamma-linolenic acid which is found in abundance in the oil of the Evening Primrose plant. The implications of this research are profound and it is advocated that Evening Primrose oil be incorporated into the programme as a source of this normal body metabolite.

It is of the greatest importance that we recognize the interdependence of the various nutrients with each other. Thus, whilst it is valid to stress that, for example a zinc or molybdenum deficient diet could predispose to one or another form of cancer, the fact remains that unless all the nutrients (some forty different substances) are present in optimum quantities, to meet the individual needs of the person, there will be some degree of impairment to the surveillance capabilities of the defensive system of the body — the immune system.

The natural defence against cancer depends largely upon that immune capability, and this in turn depends largely upon our nutritional status. The ability of the macrophages to recognize tumour cells is one part of this intrinsic anti-cancer process. A further aspect of this is the efficiency of the protein digesting enzymes, which again depends upon adequate nutrition (zinc etc.) Krebs[15] insists that over and above the immune and enzyme system's defensive role against tumour cells, there exists an extrinsic anti-neoplastic (anti-cancer) factor. This outside agent enhances the body's defence capacity. This he sees as the role of B_{17}. There is, therefore, a potential role in any prevention programme for the use of either apricot kernels or supplemental B_{17}.

The specific substances discussed, thus far, do not form a comprehensive list of all of those on which there have been reports relating to cancer. However, they should be taken as examples. If we consider those substances discussed as being among the most important in the nutritional approach to the prevention of cancer then we should obviously ensure a regular intake in our diets of those foods which contain them and which are not contra-indicated, in an anti-cancer diet.

Food Sources
The main desirable food sources of these is as follows:

Vitamin A: Dark green, leafy vegetables, yellow fruits and vegetables, eggs, liver.

B Vitamins: Wholegrains, brewer's yeast, legumes, wheatgerm, organ meats, nuts.

Vitamin C: Fruit (Citrus, cantaloupe, cherries) sprouted seeds (alfalfa), vegetables (broccoli, peppers, tomatoes).

Vitamin E: Cold pressed oils, wheatgerm, leafy vegetables, sweet potatoes, eggs.

Calcium Green, leafy vegetables (cabbage), molasses, kelp (seaweed).

Phosphorus: Legumes, nuts, wholegrains, cereals, fish.

Selenium: Brewer's yeast, wheatgerm, broccoli, wholegrains, tuna, herring, garlic.

Zinc: Pumpkin and sunflower seeds, mushrooms, brewer's yeast, soya beans, organ meats.

Molybdenum. Legumes, wholegrains, dark green vegetables.

Manganese: Wholegrains, green, leafy vegetables, legumes, nuts, pineapple, eggyolk.

Germanium: Garlic

Chromium: Wholegrains, brewer's yeast.

B_{17}: Apricot kernels, cherry, peach and plum pits, apple seeds, millet.

The suggested supplements and dosages as set out below are guidelines only. Some people will need other supplements and some will certainly require more of certain substances than the amounts given. There is no substitute for an individualized nutritional programme, tailored to the particular needs of the person involved. However as a guide, the following would be indicated in most people as a daily supplement in a prevention programme:

Vitamin A (emulsified): 25,000 iu*

*Note that if high dosages (above 50,000 iu) of vitamin A are taken by women of childbearing age, it is important that zinc, vitamin E and the B vitamin Choline, are also taken.

Vitamin B complex (containing at least 50mg each of B_3, B_6 and
  Calcium pantothenate.): 1 or 2 capsules.
Vitamin C: At least 500mg.
Vitamin E: 200 IU
Vitamin B_{17} : 3 x 25mg (or kernels + seeds).
Calcium orotate (B_{13} Calcium): 500mg.
Magnesium orotate (B_{13} Magnesium): 500mg.
Vitamin F (Cold pressed vegetable oil): 1 dessertspoonful.
Calcium pantothenate (Vitamin B_5): 100mg.
Zinc orotate (B_{13}-zinc): 100mg.
Selenium: 50mcg.
Oil of Evening Primrose (Source of Linoleic acid): 500mg.
Bromelaine enzymes: 1 or 2 x 200mg. with each meal.

This is not an exhaustive list and, as has been mentioned
before, the quantities required of the substances on the list can
vary from person to person. Other vital nutrients such as
potassium are thought by many to play a vital role in defending
the body against cancer. If, however, we use the most common
foods on the list of those which provide the bulk of the nutrients
listed above, in order to help us to form the basis of a dietary
pattern, we will find that we automatically include other factors
such as potassium (as well as sufficient fibre to obviate the need
for additional bran etc.).

Appearing most commonly as foods rich in these essential
nutrients are the following:

Dark green vegetables and fruit.
Yellow vegetables and fruit.
Wholegrain cereals (Oats, wheat, rye, millet, barley, rice).
Buckwheat.
Legumes.
Seeds (sunflower, sesame, flax or linseed, pumpkin), nuts,
sprouted seeds, seed kernels.
Eggs.
Wheatgerm.
Organ meats.
Fish
Molasses.
Garlic.

If we check against other nutrients not specifically discussed
above, such as potassium, we find that its main sources are

wholegrains, vegtables, legumes and some seeds. The same is true of all nutrients required for health. Our plan for eating should therefore include a predominance of these foods. For those who are attracted to the vegetarian ideal, the leaving out of fish and organ meats would in no way diminish the effectiveness of this health-promoting diet. Indeed many researchers (see Chapter 3) would urge the vegetarian pattern of eating as that most conducive to a cancer-free life. The recent medical conversion to the use of fibre in the diet is also catered for as this pattern of eating is a perfect high fibre diet. A reduction in bowel cancer is postulated as a result of improved bowel transit time. Toxic residues which might contain carcinogens are kept on the move in this way. Bowel stasis is a key factor in many cancer patients and tne high-fibre diet remedies this. If at the same time as adopting the regular eating of these health giving foods we also eliminate as many incriminated foods and substances from the regular part of our diet, we will have performed the two most important nutritional duties, we can, and will have improved our health prospects.

Among the undesirable substances and foods are the following:

Alcohol: Dr Roger R. Williams conducting a research programme for the National Institute for Health, in the U.S.A., discovered that alcohol consumption increases the chances of skin, breast and thyroid cancers. It seems that alcohol stimulates pituitary function which in turn speeds up cell production, and susceptibility to malignancy increases. In his book *Comprehensive Answers to Nutrition* (Published by the author, 1979) W. Borrmann D.C. describes this research as follows: 'The study consisted of 1,127 people with breast cancer, 709 people with thyroid cancer, and 89 people with melanoma (skin cancer). All forms of alcohol were involved: beer, wine and hard liquor. These people drank from as little as one drink per month to $\frac{1}{2}$ a pint a day. The study seemed to indicate that 16,000 new cases of breast cancer a year could be attributed to the use of alcohol. The study also investigated several common drugs and it seemed to indicate a connection with some of these and cancer. A separate study conducted at the University of California at Los Angeles, School of Public Health, confirms Dr Williams' findings. Dr James Enstrom, a specialist in epedemiology, agrees that alcohol may increase the susceptibility to cancer.'

The liver, our major organ of detoxification is the one most damaged by alcohol abuse, and it makes perfect sense that this cannot but be a negative factor in the effort for optimum health. There is recent evidence that a small quantity of alcohol ($1\frac{1}{2}$ wineglasses of wine daily, or its equivelant) has beneficial effects on other aspects of health, such as the heart. The anti-cancer programme would therefore minimize the use of alcohol rather than totally ban it.

A recent report in *The Lancet* confirms the previously mentioned research. (1(1982), 267 — 270) A survey of 4,373 women in the U.S.A. has shown that patients who consumed alcohol were $1\frac{1}{2}$ to 2 times more at risk of developing breast cancer than patients who never drank. Other factors (smoking, diet, drug abuse etc.) were not compared, so these and the previously mentioned surveys, are at best circumstantial links. As stated in the introduction the principles that apply to the control of existing cancer also apply to the prevention of cancer. It is only a matter of degree and emphasis.

Eggs have a high cholesterol content and no more than three should be eaten per week and not at the same meal as other animal protein food. *Cheese* can, of course, be high or low in fat, and the latter is preferable. Dutch Gouda and Edam, Greek féta (goat's cheese), Roquefort, cottage cheese and other low-fat goat or sheep cheeses are the most acceptable. Cooked cheese is highly indigestible, but Parmesan, sprinkled on hot vegetables, is quite acceptable. *Cow's milk* is fine food for baby cows but many people are sensitive to it, especially when pasteurized, and I do not recommend its use. A little skimmed milk may be used, or better still goat's milk. Cow's milk frequently contains residues of drugs used in commercial dairy farming. *Butter* is best avoided entirely. A suitable replacement would be a vegetable margarine, with unsaturated fats, or a nut butter.

Some flesh foods such as fish or lean meat, or organ meat, may be eaten two or three times a week. A little of these foods goes a long way and the introduction of vegetarian dishes, including pulses and cereals would be an advantage. The diet should be predominantly raw food orientated.

Anything containing *white flour* or *refined sugar* should be eliminated from the diet. *Smoked, pickled, preserved, salted or spicy foods* are harmful and may contain carcinogens. These should also be left out of the diet. *Salt* is known to cause chemical imbalances within the system which tend towards a pre-cancerous condition. Care should be taken regarding *baking powder (bicarbonate of soda), health salts* and *mineral water containing sodium chloride* (NaCl). Vichy water, for example, contains a massive 3.630g of bicarbonate of soda per litre, of water while Contrexville water contains a miniscule .002g per litre and would therefore be regarded as acceptable. Perrier water is also acceptable, containing a mere .024g of NaCl per litre.

It is a sad fact that few people actually look at the lists of food additives used in commercially prepared foods. Some of those commonly used have given rise to speculation as to their long-term effects on health. Whether or not specifically carcinogenic they have a tendency to reduce biochemical and biological integrity. Since our aim is to keep these aspects at an optimum it is necessary to suggest that all additive⊾ be avoided. All *colouring, flavouring, stabilizers, bleaching agents, preservatives, emulsifying agents, etc.*, should be totally avoided. This effectively rules out of a prevention diet most tinned and preserved or processed foods. Read the labels carefully, for some foods are now marketed free of all such contaminants. Interestingly, white bread contains dozens of additives.

Since obese individuals are statistically more prone to cancer it is clear that not only what, but how much we eat matters. Foods eaten should be predominantly uncooked and unprocessed. At least 60 per cent of the food in the diet should be within these catagories. Attention should be given to providing adequate protein from vegetable sources by combining at the same meal pulses (bean family) and grains (cereals) to give a supply of all the essential building blocks (amino-acids) of protein. Animal protein is not in any way essential to life or to health. If it is avoided, however, the vegetable source must be carefully incorporated into the diet.

All stimulants such as *tea, coffee, chocolate, cocoa* and *cola drinks* should be avoided.

In order to obtain an adequate amount of B17 the foods rich in this substance should be a part of the everyday eating pattern. The eating of several apples or pears daily, together with their pips, will provide a quantity of B17. If obtainable, six to eight apricot, peach or nectarine kernels can be eaten. If found palatable (the bitter taste is an aquired one) they can be ground in a nut mill or a coffee grinder and sprinkled on soup, salad or muesli.

Commercially marketed apricot pit powder is now available

and provides a good scource of B17. However, such products may have been 'defatted' which means the oil is removed, and with it an important ingredient, absisic acid. Dr James Privatera has found this to be a natural pain killer, and he recommends ten apricot kernels to be eaten daily[16].

Since the bitterness of these kernels can be an obstacle to their regular consumption, the following method, brought to my attention by my wife, might be helpful. Open the apricot, remove and crack the stone to extract the kernel. Place the kernel in the apricot and eat it and the fruit together. The bitterness of the kernel will be found to be imperceptible.

The inclusion of the various fruits listed on page 61 as well as the beans, nuts and sprouted seeds and beans, will ensure that the chance of B17 deficiency is minimized. If at the same time there is a determined effort to balance the diet and supplement programme on the lines indicated, as well as the avoiding of obvious carcinogenic factors, then all that can be done to avoid cancer, by nutritional means, will have been done. Thus far the methods appear to have succeeded.

At the moment we do not know the body's exact requirements for B17. It will doubtless prove a varying one dependent upon age, sex, state of health and of course inherited factors. What we do know is that where an abundance of these foods is taken there is no cancer. We can only urge that efforts be made to emulate the pattern of eating of the Hunza people.

Can we harm ourselves by eating foods rich in cyanide? Too much of anything is harmful. There is a case reported of a fatality resulting from the eating of a cupful of apple seeds, though this has not been authenticated. No one, however, should ever suggest the intake of such a vast amount of nitrilosides at one sitting. A golden rule should be to never eat more pits or pips at one sitting than you would eat fruit. Despite this advice it is worth noting that many people eat between twenty and fifty apricot kernels daily, with no apparent ill-effects.

General health care, such as adequate fresh air and exercise, are important.

There is ample evidence of the negative effect on health resulting from exposure to artificial light and inadequate exposure to natural light. John Ott[17] has shown the vital need of the body and especially of the eyes to have access to unimpeded natural daylight. As Ott explains: 'Light entering the eyes influences the endocrine system thereby influencing the production and release of hormones for the control of the body chemistry, along with nutrition and other factors.' This may appear at first glance to be far fetched, but extensive trials have shown profound physiological and psychological changes when normal artificial light is changed to full-spectrum light, which mimics the range of sunlight.

Recent reports also indicate that people who spend much of their working day in artificially lit areas, where fluorescent lights are used, are more prone to skin cancer.

Caution should, of course, be exercised in the degree of exposure to natural sunlight as well, especially for the cancer patient. As with all things in life, too much is often as bad as too little. Sun-bathing should be indulged in for limited periods only, say half-an-hour morning and afternoon.

The following pattern of eating is meant as a general guide. Within the framework of this diet there is the scope for much individuality and for differing tastes. The recipes which follow are meant as examples of the type, and variety, of dishes suitable for this programme of prevention and health maintenance.

Breakfast
Choose from:
Fresh fruit and seeds and nuts,
or Muesli (see recipe) and fruit,
or millet or oatmeal porridge (no salt), plus wheatgerm.
plus ¼ pint (140ml/⅔ cupful) goats yogurt.
If still hungry add wholemeal toast/bread and spread such as non-sugar jam, tahini or banana.
Drink
Herb tea, coffee substitute or mineral water.

Mid-morning
Fresh or '*Biotta*' vegetable juice, or herb tea, or a piece of fruit.

Lunch
Large mixed salad plus sprouted-seeds, nuts and seeds. Add: low fat cheese (cottage, Edam, Gouda, féta) and a jacket potato or wholemeal bread or brown rice and soya sauce. Dress with cold-pressed olive oil and lemon juice.

Dessert:
Fresh or lightly stewed fruit (honey as sweetener).

Mid–afternoon
As mid–morning .

Evening meal
Alternate days should include an animal protein (unless a vegetarian pattern has been decided on). On one night have a fish meal and the following night a vegetarian dish (pulse/cereal mixture such as lentils or soya together with rice or millet. (see recipes). The third night could include chicken or liver with a vegetarian meal on the fourth night, and so on. Fish could be eaten twice weekly, poultry once, and organ or lean meat once weekly. A variety of raw or lightly cooked vegetables should accompany whichever of these meals is being eaten. Steaming is the ideal cooking medium as it conserves essential nutrients.
Dessert:
Fruit

*   *   *

Learning to cook with herbs as the main condiment is helpful in the making of interesting and varied dishes. There is no excuse whatever for thinking that this type of eating pattern is dull. An effort and some imagination can transform it into a far more varied pattern than conventional menus. The recipes that follow are examples to get started with, and there is a fast growing range of wholefood cookery books now available from which further inspiration can be gained.

The recipes that follow carry an indication as to whether they are suitable in the prevention diet (P), or the treatment diet (T), or both (P and T). Some of the recipes are deliberately rich in B_{17} containing foods and these will carry the additional indication (+ B_{17}).

BREAKFAST RECIPE 1
Muesli (P and T + B₁₇)

Imperial/Metric	American
2 dessertspoonsful rolled oats	4 teaspoonsful rolled oats
1½ dessertspoonful sunflower seeds	3 teaspoonsful sunflower seeds
1 dessertspoonful seedless raisins	2 teaspoonsful seedless raisins
1 teaspoonful pine kernels	1 teaspoonful pine kernels
1 teaspoonful millet	1 teaspoonful millet
1 teaspoonful sesame seeds	1 teaspoonful sesame seeds
Chopped dried fruit to taste	Chopped dried fruit to taste

Soak in cold water overnight (8 to 12 hours) and just prior to eating add:

1 finely grated apple	1 finely grated apple
1 dessertspoonful wheatgerm	2 teaspoonsful wheatgerm

This is nutritious and should be chewed thoroughly.

BREAKFAST RECIPE 2
Ground and cooked Grain Breakfast (P and T + B₁₇)

Any combination of the following grains and seeds can be rapidly prepared in the manner described:

> Barley, wheat, millet, linseed, buckwheat, brown rice, rye, oats, sunflower seeds, pumpkin seeds, sesame seeds.

1. Grind selected grains and seeds in a food processor and add 2 or 3oz (55—85g/½—¾ cupful) of this mixture to 2 cupsful of cold water to which a teaspoonful of potassium chloride (salt substitute) has been added.
2. Cook on a medium heat until it thickens. Stir frequently. Five minutes is normal preparation time. Serve warm with added yogurt and/or fruit.

At Least 4 or 5 ingredients should be used for variety. If millet, linseed or buckwheat are included this adds to the B₁₇ intake.

BREAKFAST RECIPE 3
Millet, Buckwheat and Linseed (P and T + B₁₇)

1. Equal quantities of millet and buckwheat (say 1½ desserts-poonsful/3 teaspoonsful of each) plus 1 or 2 teaspoonsful of linseed should either be soaked in a little water overnight or reduced to a powder in a food processor or nut mill.
2. Add to natural yogurt or buttermilk or soya milk. Serve with fresh fruit (grated apple or peach, apricot, grapes, sliced banana etc.). Chew well.

BREAKFAST RECIPE 4
Spreads for Wholemeal Bread or Toast (P and T)

(a) Banana and Sesame Spread
    Into a food processor place a tablespoonful of sesame seeds (roasted) and a banana. Blend to a fine paste with a teaspoonful of sunflower seed oil and a touch of lemon juice.
(b) Banana (ripe) and Avocado
    Blend these together with a fork and add a little lemon juice.
(c) Banana and Almond
    Reduce a few almonds to a powder in a food processor. Add banana, 1 teaspoonful of sunflower seed oil and a touch of lemon juice and blend to a paste.

Note: The bread used should be 100 per cent wholemeal. Many excellent recipes exist for home-made bread.

BREAKFAST RECIPE 5
Nut, Seed, Fruit, Yogurt and Honey Delight (P and T)

The following recipe was devised by my wife Alkmini and is described in her book *Greek Vegetarian Cooking*. It was originally meant for infants but makes an excellent and nutritious meal which is easily eaten and digested by anyone with chewing or swallowing difficulties. It makes a good breakfast but can be eaten at any time of day.

Imperial (Metric)	American
1 walnut	1 English walnut
4 almonds	4 almonds
1 teaspoonful sunflower and/or pumpkin seeds	1 teaspoonful sunflower and/or pumpkin seeds
½ peach, nectarine, apple or pear	½ peach, nectarine, apple or pear
4 grapes	4 grapes
¼ avocado pear	¼ avocado pear
½ banana	½ banana
1 dessertspoonful pure honey	2 teaspoonsful pure honey
½ carton natural goat's yogurt	½ carton natural goat's yogurt

1. Reduce the nuts and seeds to a powder in a food processor, or grate finely in a grinder.
2. The fruit should be grated and *puréed* in a processor and mixed with the powdered or ground nut and seed mixture together with the honey and yogurt.

Salads

Since the eating of raw vegetables must play a large part in the treatment and prevention of cancer it is desirable for there to be a reasonable variety of salads available in order to ring the changes and maintain interest and excitement in the food. The first four salads are adapted from *Greek Vegetarian Cooking*.

SALAD RECIPE 1
Greek Peasant Salad (P and T)

Imperial (Metric)	American
2—3 radishes	2—3 radishes
2 tomatoes, thinly sliced	2 tomatoes, thinly sliced
8 slices cucumber	8 slices cucumber
½ green pepper, thinly chopped	½ green bell pepper, thinly chopped
2 lettuce leaves, shredded	2 lettuce leaves, shredded
2 spring onions, sliced	2 scallions, sliced
½ onion, sliced	½ onion, sliced
2 dessertspoonsful chopped parsley	4 teaspoonsful chopped parsley

Dressing:

½ teaspoonful oregano	½ teaspoonful oregano
5 dessertspoonsful olive oil	¼ cupful olive oil
Lemon juice to taste	Lemon juice to taste
4oz (115g) féta or other white cheese, or tofu	1 cupful féta or other white cheese or tofu
Black olives	Black olives

1. Wash all salad ingredients prior to preparation. Then place them in a bowl.
2. Prepare the dressing and pour it over the salad.
3. Mix gently with a wooden serving set. Add crumbled or diced cheese and olives.
4. Serve with a jacket potato or wholemeal bread or rice savoury.

Note: In treatment programme leave out the cheese.

SALAD RECIPE 2
Lettuce Salad (P and T)

Imperial (Metric)	**American**
1 fresh firm lettuce	1 fresh firm lettuce
4 spring onions	4 scallions
5 mint leaves and/or	5 mint leaves and/or
⅓ cupful chopped parsley	⅓ cupful chopped parsley

Dressing:

3 tablespoonsful olive oil	3 tablespoonsful olive oil
2 tablespoonsful lemon juice	2 tablespoonsful lemon juice
Potassium chloride	Potassium chloride
(salt substitute)	(salt substitute)

1. Wash the vegetables and tear the lettuce by hand into small pieces.
2. Chop the other ingredients and place in a bowl. Add dressing and serve.

SALAD RECIPE 3
Dandelion, Radish and Radish Top Salad (P and T)

Imperial (Metric)	**American**
15 young dandelion leaves, chopped	15 young dandelion leaves, chopped
6 radishes and radish tops, chopped	6 radishes and radish tops, chopped
1 small onion, sliced	1 small onion, sliced

Dressing:

2 tablespoonsful olive oil	2 tablesponsful olive oil
1½ dessertspoonsful lemon juice	3 teaspoonsful lemon juice
Potassium chloride	Potassium chloride
(salt substitute)	(salt substitute)

Place the ingredients into a bowl, add the dressing, mix thoroughly and serve.

SALAD RECIPE 4
Raw Artichoke Salad (P and T)

Artichokes are delicious eaten raw. They are rich in minerals and are reputed to aid liver function. They may be used raw in salads. Remove all of the leaves and the 'beard' covering the heart. Rub with lemon juice to prevent discoloration and then dice the heart.

Imperial (Metric)	American
1 artichoke heart, diced	1 artichoke heart, diced
1 stick celery, skinned and diced	1 stalk celery, skinned and diced
1 tomato, sliced	1 tomato, sliced
6 tender dandelion leaves, chopped	6 tender dandelion leaves, chopped
2 spring onions, chopped	2 scallions, chopped
Olives (optional)	Olives (optional)

Dress with a generous amount of olive oil, lemon juice and salt substitute.

SALAD RECIPE 5
Rice Salad (P and T)

Imperial (Metric)

½ cupful cooked brown rice (cold)

½ cupful fresh peeled and chopped peaches or apples

2 sticks celery, finely chopped

½ green pepper, finely chopped

¼ onion, chopped

½oz (15g) sunflower seeds

½oz (15g) chopped raisins

Salt substitute

2 dessertspoonsful olive oil or sunflower seed oil

Lemon juice to taste

1 teaspoonful soya sauce

1 teaspoonful honey

1 tablespoonful chopped parsley

American

¾ cupful cooked brown rice (cold)

¾ cupful fresh peeled and chopped peaches or apples

2 stalks celery, finely chopped

½ green bell pepper, finely chopped

¼ onion, chopped

2 tablespoonsful sunflower seeds

2 tablespoonsful chopped raisins

Salt substitute

4 teaspoonsful olive oil or sunflower seed oil

Lemon juice to taste

1 teaspoonful soy sauce

1 teaspoonful honey

1 tablespoonful chopped parsley

Mix all ingredients gently but throroughly and serve.

*   *   *

The mixing together of a selection of raw vegetables is one definition of a salad. In this regard, all of the following can be eaten raw in salads. The greater the variety the greater the degree of interest and the more pleasure and nutrient value there will be.

Carrots, lettuce, cucumber, tomatoes, artichoke, dandelion, sprouted seeds, fennel, kale, chives, chicory, white and red cabbage, radish, avocado pear, mustard and cress, nasturtium leaves, mushrooms, leeks, broccoli, peppers, cauliflower, green peas, parsley, mint, endive, turnips, garlic, kohl rabi, watercress, spinach, green beans, brussels sprouts, parsnips, beetroot, etc.

All root vegetables, such as raw beetroot and carrot, should be prepared by grating them on the finest part of the grater as close to meal time as possible to avoid undue nutrient loss through oxidation. A few drops of lemon juice may be added (for example) to grated carrot or grated raw beetroot. Use herbs such as mint, garlic and parsley generously to enhance salads and heighten flavours.

*   *   *

SALAD RECIPE 6
Basic Coleslaw (P and T)

Imperial (Metric)	American
2 cupsful shredded white cabbage	2¼ cupsful shredded white cabbage
1 apple, shredded	1 apple, shredded
1 carrot, shredded or grated	1 carrot, shredded or grated
1 onion, shredded	1 onion, shredded

Dressing:

1 dessertspoonful sunflower seed oil	2 teaspoonsful sunflower seed oil
Chopped parsley	Chopped parsley
2 teaspoonsful lemon juice	2 teaspoonsful lemon juice
A little water	A little water

1.   Mix the fruit and vegetable ingredients well together.
2.   Make up the dressing, pour over the salad and serve.

SALAD RECIPE 7
Mixed Salad (P)

A selection of any five or six items on the list above should be decoratively arranged so that there is a contrast of colours and textures. The sight of an all green salad is lightened and made more exciting to the palate by the addition of a few touches of red (radish, red pepper) or orange (carrot).

One grated raw vegetable, some of the coleslaw mixture or one of recipes Nos. 2, 3, 4 or 5, plus one or two green salad vegetables (watercress, chicory) and a sprinkling of seeds and nuts as well as some sprouting seeds (mung beans, alfalfa) plus a light dressing (which can include olive oil, lemon juice, crushed garlic, yogurt) and/or the addition of herbs such as mint or parsley, will present the taste senses with a feast of flavours.

There is no end to the variety available. Depending upon seasonal changes and economic factors salads are always possible and should always be interesting and enjoyable.

If chewing is a problem ingredients can be liquidized or juiced. There is some loss of value in such cases unless immediately consumed, though. The Gerson Therapy method incorporates the drinking of large amounts of freshly prepared juices as well as the eating of raw salads.

Cooked Recipes
The objective of this section is to present a few examples of dishes which are nutritious and which supply complete proteins mainly from non-animal sources. Remember that by combining grains and pulses this essential target is achieved.

COOKED RECIPE 1
Lentil and Nut Loaf (P)

Imperial (Metric)	American
½lb (225g) Continental lentils	1 cupful Continental lentils
5oz (140g) wholemeal bread-crumbs or cooked millet	2 cupsful wholewheat bread-crumbs or cooked millet
1 large onion, chopped	1 large onion, chopped
8 cloves of garlic (whole)	8 cloves of garlic (whole)
3 tablespoonsful olive oil	3 tablespoonsful olive oil
1½ teaspoonsful oregano	1½ teaspoonsful oregano
5oz (140g) ground walnuts or almonds and/or pine kernels	1 cupful ground English walnuts or almonds and/or pine kernels
3 tablespoonsful chopped parsley	3 tablespoonsful chopped parsley
2 tablespoonsful tomato *purée*	2 tablespoonsful tomato paste
2 eggs	2 eggs
Salt substitute	Salt substitute
Freshly ground black pepper	Freshly ground black pepper

1. Soak lentils for several hours. Rinse and place in saucepan cover in cold water. Simmer for 20 minutes until tender. Drain surplus water.
2. Fry onions and garlic in oil until lightly brown. Remove from heat and add nuts, lentils, breadcrumbs, tomato *purée*, oregano, parsley and eggs. Mix well and add salt substitute and pepper.
3. Line a loaf tin with tin foil and grease with oil. Place mixture in tin and cover with greased foil. Bake in oven at 350°F/180°C (Gas Mark 4) for about an hour. After removing from oven allow to cool for a few minutes before taking out of tin.
4. Serve thick slices with vegetables or salad, garnished with tomato, parsley and onion.

COOKED RECIPE 2
Bean Pilaff (P and T)

Imperial (Metric)

1 cupful brown rice or millet
2oz (55g) cooked beans
  (red, blackeyed, haricot,
  broad, etc.)
1 stick celery, chopped
1 leek, sliced
1 onion, diced
2oz (55g) sultanas

American

1¼ cupful brown rice or
  millet
¼ cupful cooked beans
  (red, blackeyed, navy,
  Windsor, etc.)
1 stalk celery, chopped
1 leek, sliced
1 onion, diced
⅓ cupful golden seedless
  raisins

1. Boil all ingredients (except beans which should be prepared separately) in a little water (1 to 1½ cupsful) until tender.
2. Add cooked beans and serve with mixed cooked vegetables and a dressing of olive oil. Garnish with parsley.

COOKED RECIPE 3
Butter Beans and Millet (or Rice) and Vegetables (P and T)

Imperial (Metric)
¾ cupful butter beans
½ cupful brown rice or millet
2 leeks, chopped
1 medium or large tomato, chopped
1 onion, chopped
2 carrots, chopped
1 stick celery, chopped
2 dessertspoonsful olive oil
Salt substitute

American
1 cupful lima beans
¾ cupful brown rice or millet
2 leeks, chopped
1 medium or large tomato, chopped
1 onion chopped
2 carrots, chopped
1 stalk celery, chopped
4 teaspoonsful olive oil
Salt substitute

1. Soak butter beans overnight.
2. Simmer for 45 minutes and then add all the vegetables as well as the salt substitute and the oil. Cover with water and simmer until water has evaporated.

COOKED RECIPE 4
Lentils, Millet and Vegetables (P and T)

Imperial (Metric)
½ cupful lentils
½ cupful millet
2 carrots, chopped
½ onion, chopped
1 tomato, chopped
1 small potato,
   scrubbed and chopped
2 tablespoonsful olive oil
⅓ teaspoonful oregano
Salt substitute

American
¾ cupful lentils
¾ cupful millet
2 carrots, chopped
½ onion, chopped
1 tomato, chopped
1 small potato,
   scrubbed and chopped
2 tablespoonsful olive oil
⅓ teaspoonful oregano
Salt substitute

1. Prepare the lentils by soaking overnight and rinsing well.
2. Place soaked and rinsed lentils into a saucepan with 1 pint (½ litre/2½ cupful) water. Add all other ingredients and simmer until water has evaporated.
3. Serve with cooked vegetables or salad.

COOKED RECIPE 5
Chickpeas, Millet (or Rice) and Vegetables (P and T)

Imperial (Metric)
¾ cupful chickpeas
1 cupful millet (or brown rice)
2 tablespoonsful olive oil
⅓ teaspoonful rosemary
1 tomato, chopped
2 carrots, chopped
Salt substitute

American
1 cupful garbanzo beans
1¼ cupful millet (or rice)
2 tablespoonsful olive oil
⅓ teaspoonful rosemary
1 tomato, chopped
2 carrots, chopped
Salt substitute

1. Soak chickpeas (garbanzo beans) overnight and rinse.
2. Cook soaked and rinsed chickpeas (garbanzo beans) until tender, then add all the vegetables and millet (or pre-cooked brown rice) and salt substitute. Cover with water and simmer until water has evaporated.
3. Serve with fresh vegetables or salad.

COOKED RECIPE 6
Spinach, Rice, Chickpeas and Vegetables (P and T)

Imperial (Metric)	American
1lb (455g) spinach	2 cupsful spinach
½ cupful brown rice	¾ cupful brown rice
¾ cupful chickpeas	1 cupful garbanzo beans
2 carrots	2 carrots
1 clove garlic or	1 clove garlic or 3 scallions
3 spring onions	2 tablespoonsful olive oil
2 tablespoonsful olive oil	Salt substitute
Salt substitute	

1. Soak the chickpeas (garbanzo beans) overnight.
2. Change the water and cook chickpeas (garbanzo beans) until tender. Add brown rice and part cook this (15 minutes) before adding all other ingredients. Cover with water and simmer until water has evaporated.
3. Serve with cooked vegetables or salad.

*   *   *

Cooked recipes 3, 4 and 5 may be reduced to a *purée*, after cooking, for anyone with chewing difficulties, or for young children.

*   *   *

Soups

It is not difficult to see how the combining of pulses and cereals is facilitated by incorporating them into a soup. This is also an easy way of eating food if the appetite is less than at its best.

SOUP RECIPE 1
Lentil Soup (P and T)

Imperial (Metric)	American
¾lb (340g) lentils	1½ cupsful lentils
1 large carrot, chopped	1 large carrot, chopped
8 cloves garlic, halved lengthwise	8 cloves garlic, halved lengthwise
½ onion, chopped	½ onion, chopped
½ teaspoonful oregano	½ teaspoonful oregano
½ cupful olive oil	¾ cupful olive oil
1 large tin peeled tomatoes, sieved	1 large can peeled tomatoes, sieved
Salt substitute (to taste)	Salt substitute (to taste)
Freshly ground black pepper (to taste)	Freshly ground black pepper (to taste)

1. Boil the lentils for five minutes, strain and add to 2 pints (1 litre/5 cupsful) water. Bring to boil and allow to simmer a further 15 minutes.
2. Add all other ingredients and allow to cook on low heat for about an hour.
3. When ready the soup should be thick, but not solid. Add more water if required.
4. Eat with toast and a stick of fresh celery.

SOUP RECIPE 2
Chickpea Soup (P and T)

Imperial (Metric)
1lb (455g) chickpeas
¾ cupful olive oil
2 tablespoonsful rosemary
Salt substitute
Freshly ground black pepper
Lemon juice

American
2 cupsful garbanzo beans
1 cupful olive oil
2 tablespoonsful rosemary
Salt substitute
Freshly ground black pepper
Lemon juice

1. Soak chickpeas (garbanzo beans) for 24 hours, changing water at least twice.
2. Simmer them for 30 minutes, change water and simmer for a further 20 minutes before changing water again.
3. Add rosemary, salt substitute, pepper and oil and allow to simmer until chickpeas (garbanzo beans) are very tender.
4. Add a squeeze of lemon juice prior to serving.

SOUP RECIPE 3
Bean Soup (P and T)

Imperial (Metric)	American
¾lb (340g) haricot beans	1½ cupsful navy beans
1 leek, chopped	1 leek, chopped
2 carrots, chopped	2 carrots, chopped
2 onions, chopped	2 onions, chopped
3 stalks celery, chopped	3 stalks celery, chopped
1 large tin tomatoes	1 large can tomatoes
¾ cupful olive oil	1 cupful olive oil
Salt substitute	Salt substitute
Freshly ground black pepper	Freshly ground black pepper

1. Soak beans overnight.
2. Rinse well and place in saucepan with water and bring to boil. Allow to cook for 15 minutes before changing water. Bring to boil again and leave to simmer until beans show signs of splitting.
3. Add all vegetables, and add salt and pepper to taste. Also, add more water if necessary and allow to simmer until all vegetables are tender.

The thickness of soup is a matter of taste and more or less water can be added to achieve the desired consistency.

Note: The procedure of soaking, cooking and changing water in the bean and chickpea recipes is to ensure that enzymes present in their skins have been leached away. Otherwise the familiar 'bloating' which follows the eating of members of the bean family will be all too obvious. Also of course this procedure ensures tender end results in the cooking.

*   *   *

The foregoing examples, plus an animal protein meal on alternate days, and the use of fresh fruit, seeds and nuts should enable a more than reasonable pattern of eating to be enjoyed by the most amateur of cooks. By exploring the various cookbooks on wholefood, vegetarian and vegan cooking and adapting where necessary it should be possible to provide the variety and interest as well as the nutritive value required to conform to the programme suggested herein.

Since all the evidence points to cancer being preventable for most people it makes sense to work towards the goal of health by removing negative environmental factors which can be cancer causing. If life is worth living then it is worth living well. The quality of life can be vastly improved by the self same methods which also provide a shield against cancer.

Cancer is increasing in young people, it is increasing in middle-aged people, and it is increasing in the elderly. Everything we do that improves health, protects against cancer. Our diet and general habits of life are those major areas over which we have some control. If it is important to live in a good state of health then there is little doubt that we can help this by our own efforts. Of course there are those who will talk of a 'short life and a merry one' or those who feel that it is all too difficult. Perhaps a subconscious death-wish prevails in such people, or perhaps their way of thinking reflects the nihilism and despair of modern living. For those who wish to make the effort the rewards are in proportion to the effort made. For those planning families it should be important to ensure that the next generation starts with a better chance of survival than the last. Noxious substances present in the mother can be passed to the infant in the mother's milk. Surely it is the expectant mothers responsibility to ensure that she feeds her offspring healthy milk.

We cannot cheat nature's response. If we do those things that are bound to lead to disease then we must expect to become diseased. It is no good expecting a miraculous reprieve from the consequences of our actions. Cancer is the end result of all that we do to ourselves and all that we eat. We are the cause of our own disease, we can also be the cause of our own good health.

[1] Linus Pauling, *Vitamin C and the Common Cold*, Ballantine Books, 1972.

[2] Cheraskin, Ringsdorf and Clark, *Diet and Disease,* Keats.

[3] J. Bland, *Orthomolecular Review.*.

[4] Fred Rohe, *Metabolic Ecology: a Way to Win the Cancer War*, Wedgeston Press, 1982.

[5] R. Shekell, *Orthomolecular Review*, July 1982.

[6] J. Kirschmann, *Nutrition Almanac*, McGraw Hill, 1979.

[7] J. Marks, *A Guide to All the Vitamins*, MTP, 1979

[8] *Journal of Orthomolecular Psychiatry*, 11 (1982), 28—41.

[9] F. Kalz and A. Schafer, 'Vitamin A Serum Levels After Ingestion of Different Vitamin A Preparations', *Journal of Canadian Medical Association*, 79 (1959), 918.

[10] A. Hoffer and M. Walker, *Orthomolecular Nutrition*, Keats, 1978.
[11] J. Kirschmann, *Nutrition Almanac*, McGraw Hill, 1979.
[12] *Journal of Orthomolecular Psychiatry*, 11 (1982), 28–41.
Paavo Airola, *The Miracle of Garlic*, Health Plus Publishers.
[14] Diepenaar et al, *South African Medical Journal*, 62 (1982), 505.
[15] E. Krebs Jr, *Journal of applied Nutrition*, Vol. 22, Nos. 3 and 4, pp 74–86 (1970).
[16] *Cancer Control Journal*, Vol. 3, No. 3 (1975).
[17] J. Ott, *Cancer Control Journal*, Vol. 3, No. 6 (1976).

6

Supplements
for the Cancer Patient

The role of supplements falls into two categories in the biological approach to cancer. There are those which will apply to all cases, but which may vary in dosage, depending on individual variations; there are also supplements which will only apply to selected cases. The description of these supplements must therefore not be taken to indicate that they will all be necessary in all instances.

The first of the supplements which is always indicated is Laetrile. As has already been described this is a concentrated extract of one of the nitrilosides (amygdalin, prunasin, dhurrin), also called vitamin B_{17}.

Laetrile can be administered by injection into the veins or muscles or it can be taken by mouth. Richardson gives high doses (up to nine grams daily) by injection for three weeks and then reduces the injections to 3 grams, three times weekly, for four weeks. This is then reduced to three grams, twice weekly, for a further month. A maintenance injection (still of three grams) is given once weekly for up to another eighteen months. During all this time up to two grams of Laetrile are taken orally on each day that the patient is not receiving an injection.

Moolenburgh, on rare occasions, uses intravenous administration of Laetrile, but as a rule he prescribes one gram daily to be taken morning and evening, with food, whereas Nieper uses Laetrile as a compound which also includes zinc and thyroid extract. This is usually taken in tablet form at a strength of two to three grams of Laetrile daily.

My own recommendation is that one to two grams be taken daily by mouth as tablet or powder. Never more than one gram at any one time and it is suggested that this be with or after a meal.

Moolenburgh states that 'Laetrile is one of the most non-toxic compounds I have ever come across: the secret is to give enough.'[1] There is no reference in the available literature to any pharmacologically harmful toxicity to human beings resulting from the administration of Laetrile in recommended dosages.

Griffin, in his book *World Without Cancer* quotes Dr D. Greenberg, Emeritus Professor of Biochemistry at the University of California at Berkeley, as stating 'There is no question that pure amygdalin (Laetrile) is a non-toxic compound. This is not questioned by anyone who has studied the reports submitted to the Cancer Advisory Council of the State of California'. The question of the non-toxic quality of Laetrile will be further discussed in the chapter dealing with the Laetrile controversy.

The next supplement essential to the cancer patient is protein-digesting (proteolytic) enzymes. Richardson recommends two to four pancreatic enzyme tablets to be taken four times daily. Moolenburgh prescribes bromelaine (pineapple extract) to be taken with Laetrile. He maintains that this enhances the potency of the Laetrile. Kelley insists that bromelaine should be used as an aid to digestion but that to be effective in treating cancer, pancreatic enzymes should also be used. He advises six pancreatin tablets (± 300mg each) after each meal.

Nieper recommends 600 to 1200mg of bromelaine to be taken daily. These enzymes are effective in breaking down the shield which protects the cancer cell from the body's defence mechanism. It is an extremely important aspect of the therapy.[2]

My own recommendation varies with the condition of the patient. However, the following pattern is usually advised. Before meals, tablets containing trypsin and chymotrypsin (pancreatic enzymes) should be taken as well as bromelaine or papaya enzyme. At the end of each meal half a gram of pancreatic enzyme powder should be taken. Issels, Moolenburgh and Nieper, in addition to those methods of enzyme administration, also prescribe a suppository which releases enzymes, to be used at night.

The only side effect that might be noticed with a rapid 'de-shielding' of the cancer cells, would be a shivering or slight palpitation. In such a case a reduction in the quantity of enzyme used should correct the tendency to react in this way.

Kelley points out that the patient may overload the system

with waste materials if tumour destruction is too rapid. Symptoms of nausea may result. In such cases he recommends a break of five days without enzymes, every ten days. After several such cycles he suggests a gradual return to constant taking of enzymes. As he states, 'We are not interested in getting rid of the tumour too quickly; the tumour should not be removed faster than the body can rebuild healthy tissues.'

Coffee Enema

An effective aid to the liver during such a detoxification crisis is the use of a coffee enema, and the following method is advocated whenever there is a feeling of nausea or general 'seediness'. Up to six coffee enemas may be used daily. The after-effect is usually a feeling of relief, lightness and renewed energy, and an absence of the nausea. The coffee is rapidly absorbed into the portal circulation from where it travels to the liver, causing a 'flushing' of bile, which carries with it toxic wastes.

Equipment required includes: a gravity feed enema kit; plastic sheeting; K-Y jelly; tissues.

Fresh ground (never instant) coffee is needed. Add 3 tablespoonsful to 1 litre of water. Boil for three minutes and then simmer for a further 15 minutes. Allow to cool, strain and store. Use $\frac{1}{2}$ to $\frac{3}{4}$ of a pint for each enema, which should be administered at blood heat. Ensure that bowels have moved prior to enema being used.

Arrange the equipment so that the container (with coffee solution in it) is suspended some feet above the position in which the patient is lying. The patient should be lying on his or her left side, on the plastic sheet. The end of the tube, which has been lubricated with K-Y jelly, should be inserted into the rectum and the coffee slowly allowed to drain, with gravity, into the lower bowel. When all the coffee has been absorbed the patient should remain resting for 5 to 15 minutes. Gently knead the abdomen if any discomfort is felt. After several minutes the patient should turn on to his or her right side and lie with knees bent. The enema can be voided at any time after 5 minutes of retention.

As I have said, this apparently curious method has distinctly beneficial effects and many of those who have had to use it when in some distress due to detoxification bear witness to its efficacy.

Nieper indicates that some digestive irritation can result from the prolonged use of enzymes. This does not appear to occur with the use of bromelaine or papaya enzyme.

The next essential supplement in this scheme of treatment is vitamin E. Dr Wilfrid Shute, the formost expert in the therapeutic use of vitamin E, has shown that patients on high vitamin E supplementation appear to develop cancer at a markedly lower rate than other patients.

The relationship between the rate at which a cell breathes (its respiration) and the degree of its malignancy was established by Warburg, the double Nobel prize winner. He maintained that cancer cells developed after an initial interference with the respiration of normal cells. This, he stated, could be the result of any number of chemical or physical factors. The result of this causes many cells to die. Some cells, however, adapt to a diminished oxygen supply by altering their means of survival. This is achieved by replacing the lost oxygen with energy derived from fermentation. What is certain is that the cancer cell seems to be capable of surviving and reproducing without using oxygen in the way normal cells do. Vitamin E plays a role in the utilization of oxygen. Experiments[3] have shown that tumours induced in animals were significantly smaller in those that received large amounts of vitamin E. The vitamin was shown to control the exuberant growth in chicken sarcoma. A daily intake of between 800mg and 1500mg of vitamin E is recommended.

With vitamin E it is suggested that a selenium supplement also be taken — 50 to 100mcg is the usual dosage. Selenium is under review for its anti-cancer potential and acts synergistically with vitamin E. A further anti-tumour factor which is part of the normal economy of the body is Gama Linolenic Acid (GLA), a substance which the body converts from linoleic acid.[4] Research has shown that whilst linoleic acid has no anti-tumour effect, GLA does and it is thought that part of the cancer process could involve a blockage, which prevents GLA from being formed. Since GLA is found in abundance in the Evening Primrose plant it is suggested that 3 x 500mg of oil of Evening Primrose be added to the programme.

Vitamin C is recommended in doses of between 750mg and ten grammes daily. Dr Linus Pauling, another Nobel prize winner, has shown this vitamin to be of value in cancer therapy. The importance of vitamin C to general body health, wound healing and stress makes it a vital ingredient in the therapeutic programme.

Vitamin A is thought to have a normalizing effect on hormonal balance. Moerman, as quoted by Moolenburgh,[5] prescribes between 130,000 international units and three million units daily. In these high doses emulsified vitamin A is used, since the usually obtainable oily vitamin A, in such high doses, would cause severe reactions. Doses of up to, approximately, 100,000 iu daily may consist of oily vitamin A, but not higher doses. Very high dosages could have severe side effects and on no account should such quantities be taken without expert advice. The minimum daily requirement of this vitamin is put at 5,000 ius daily. Foods such as carrots, chicory, dried apricots, dandelion, spinach, and turnip tops contain large quantities of this vital factor. It is worth stressing that the assimilation of vitamin A from vegetables is assisted by light cooking. My recommendation is that a gradual increase in vitamin A supplement intake be instituted. Starting with 50,000 units daily the patient should increase the dose by 10,000 units daily, each week, up to 130,000 units daily or until there is any indication of side effects, such as slight yellowing of the skin of the palms of the hands. Side–effects are seldom if ever serious[6] and a reduction in intake will lead to speedy normalization of these symptoms. Higher doses should not be taken unless specifically instructed.

A number of the vitamin B complex group are often recommended individually as follows:

Vitamin B1 (thiamine) up to 50mg daily (Moolenburgh suggests 100mg daily).

Vitamin B2 (riboflavin) 10mg three times daily.

Vitamin B3 (niacin or nicotinic acid) between 300mg and 3g daily, depending on the condition of the patient. Excess of this vitamin can cause a hot, flushing sensation which is not harmful but might be distressing. (This does not occur if B3 is taken in the form of nicotinamide.) This vitamin is especially useful as one of its actions is as an anti-depressant.

Vitamin B6 (pyridoxine) up to 60mg daily, depending on indications.

Pantothenic acid (calcium pantothenate) between 10mg and 3g daily are suggested depending on the general state of the patient.

Vitamin B15 (pangamic acid) is also useful in the treatment of all diseases relating to the ageing process. It assists oxygen supply to the tissues, $\frac{1}{2}$g-3g daily are recommended.

These vitamins are part of the regime recommended by Richardson, Kelley and others. Gerson, however, cautions that we must not expect the body, burdened with cancer, to react as a normal body would react to vitamin therapy. He however maintains that niacin (vitamin B₃) should be given to the cancer patient at a rate of six daily administrations of 50mg each. The side-effect that is usually experienced of redness and heat passes in a matter of minutes and should cause no concern to the patient. These tablets are best taken after a meal or drink.

In order to slow down the rate of division of the cancer cells and to improve the respiration of these cells it is now known that copper is of importance. The development of cancer is characterized by the extrusion of copper from the malignant cells. It has been shown that if copper can be transported back to these tissues the respiration rises and the rate of cell division slows down. Nieper recommends the taking of copper orotate since the molecule of orotic acid (vitamin B₁₃) has a high affinity to cancer cells. This is entirely non-toxic. Since the best effect of Laetrile and all nitrilosides on cancer cells is when they are relatively slow growing and when the respiration is high copper retro-transportation will enhance Laetrile's effectiveness.

Depending upon the particular condition of the patient various other minerals and nutritional supplements are also considered necessary.

It is almost always found to be essential to increase the intake of potassium and magnesium.* Nieper, Gerson and others consider this to be of great importance. Gerson points out that making up a deficiency of potassium in a healthy body can take months and in a seriously ill body up to a year or more may be required. An excellent method of increasing the intake of potassium is to use a 10 per cent solution of minerals of this group (potassium gluconate, potassium acetate, potassium phosphate) added to fresh apple and carrot juice.

Some additional needs might be phosphorus, zinc,* iron,* calcium,* amino-acid tablets (protein), brewer's yeast (as a source of vitamin B complex), comfrey and others. In order to assess these needs a number of tests may be required, including whole-blood analysis. Each patient will require individual consideration. The basic pattern however does not vary. This is

---

*Minerals such as these should always be taken in the form of orotates or in a chelated form if possible.

diet, Laetrile, enzymes, vitamins and minerals.

A number of the Continental experts use a variety of methods to stimulate the body into activity against the cancer cells. These include vaccination with serums made up of various of the body's own 'juices', such as blood or urine, or of actual cancerous cells.

Also widely used is BCG vaccine, a weakened tuberculosis virus, the purpose of which is to stimulate the production of white blood cells. But, as we now know, this could only be helpful to the body in its effort against the cancer cells if some method was also available for it to break through the shield which protects them from attack. This can be accomplished by proteolytic enzymes or Laetrile.

In an effort to slow down cell division and enhance respiration it is also thought to be desirable to artificially raise the temperature of the body. This is called 'fever' therapy and may involve tablets, injections or both. Another way of achieving this is to give the patient hyperthermic baths. Almost total immersion for about an hour in a bath which is slowly heated to 41°C (105°F) is the usual pattern. Cancer cells are damaged at 39°C (102°F) and destroyed at 42°C (107°F) whereas normal cells are undamaged at 43°C (109°F). The effect of Laetrile is more marked when used in conjunction with hyperthermic baths. These methods complement the effect of the supplemental therapy but should never be attempted without supervision under expert direction.

What is being attempted is the detoxification of the body, the regeneration of the various processes, the destruction, absorption and elimination of the cancer mass and the healing of organs and tissues impaired by the disease, especially the liver. This task *is* possible. That this is the only sane approach to cancer should be without doubt. No absolute certainty of success is possible in any given case, there are too many variables. However, it is within the framework outlined in this book that the patient's best chance for a real recovery from cancer lies. We will now go on to consider the current orthodox approach to cancer in its various forms. Criticism of methods must not be taken to indicate criticism of individuals or professions. Let us now investigate the various techniques used by orthodox medicine in its battle with cancer.

[1] Personal communication to the author, 1977.

[2] H. Neiper, 'Experience with Non-Toxic Cancer Therapies', paper delivered to German Society for Medical Tumour Therapy, Baden-Baden, 1976.

[3] F. Bicknell and F. Prescott, *The Vitamins in Medicine,* Heinemann Medical, 1953.

[4] Diepenaar et al., *South African Medical Journal* 62 (1982), 505 and 683.

[5] Lecture to Cancer Control Group, Worthing, 1978.

[6] Ruth Adams, *The Complete Guide to all the Vitamins*, Larchmont Books.

7

The Orthodox
Treatment of Cancer

Nothing that is said regarding current practice in the field of
cancer research and treatment should be taken to indicate
criticsm of those involved in this area of scientific endeavour.
There is no question as to the probity, dedication and integrity
of the research workers, surgeons, scientists, radiologists and
physicians whose efforts are directed towards the eradication of
this scourge. What will be questioned is the wisdom of the lines
of research being followed and the value of the methods of
treatment currently in use. Lest the motives behind this icono-
clastic approach be misunderstood it should be stated that the
only desire is to see clarity of thought and a logical approach
brought to bear on a highly emotive subject. If the arguments
put forward in this chapter are found to be unsound then let the
critics spell out precisely in what detail and degree they are
wanting.

The present ability of the medical profession to control cancer
is basically unsatisfactory. Even when we include those cases
where early recognition of the disease has been achieved, the
statistical chance of a normal life expectancy is only approximately one in three. The various current medical methods will
be analyzed individually. Certainly some cases can be made for
all of these methods, to a greater or lesser degree. The evidence
overall, however, incorporating all methods, is not encouraging. Individual cases may improve and survive whichever
method is used but the vast majority do not. In certain types of
cancer (notably skin cancer) the rate of cure and long-term survival is relatively high. It is only when these cases are included
in the general picture that we even reach a cure rate of one in
three.

Before considering the orthodox methods used to combat

cancer, it would be as well to consider, in general terms, what they are trying to achieve and what the nature of the enemy is.

Cancer must be considered to have taken a fairly long period to develop. There is general agreement that prior to active manifestation of malignancy there is a pre-cancerous stage. The boundary, therefore, between having cancer and not having cancer is a vague one. Many pre-cancerous and even early cancerous conditions never develop fully. This is confirmed by autopsies which have shown between 20 and 30 per cent of the deceased to have had undetected cancers which were in no way responsible for, or involved with, their deaths. Cancer, therefore, often has quite distant origins. Logically, measures to deal with it effectively should take into account the long-term aetiology of the disease.

Furthermore, it is reasonable to consider the general state of health of the patient. The nature of cancer suggests a breakdown of the body's defence mechanism. Attention to assisting the restoration of this vital factor would therefore seem to be an essential aspect of any method aimed at the long-term survival of the patient. It must be self-evident that if no attempt is made to enhance the defence mechanism and nothing is done to avoid those factors which predisposed the individual to the disease, then the chances of the disease recurring are great. Anything that is done to the patient in the way of treatment should not further deplete the ability of the body to combat disease. All treatment, philosophically speaking, should be free of negative side-effects. In practice this must mean that methods that suppress the ability of the body to react against foreign organisms or substances, cannot be considered helpful, whatever their short-term affect on the tumour.

The tumour mass or growth is not in itself, the disease. It is the most obvious symptom of a diseased body. The aim most often adopted in research and treatment is to reduce the tumour size or eradicate it altogether. Since it is not simply a case of reducing or removing the tumour that will determine survival for the patient, this criterion will be seen to be inadequate. Richardson terms this a 'lump and bump' approach. The long-term survival of the patient depends not on the absence or otherwise of the tumour but on the ability of the body to deal effectively with the whole process. If the results of current practice were good, or even satisfactory, then the necessity for these first thoughts would not exist. Results are not good and the reasons are not hard to see. The symptoms are being attacked and the causes ignored.

The number of women surviving five years after surgery for breast cancer is 50 per cent.[1] This is irrespective of the type of surgical intervention: whether the whole breast and the lymph nodes were removed or whether just the tumour was excised, makes no overall difference. The longer-term outlook for breast cancer patients receiving surgical treatment is less hopeful. Only 16 per cent will survive for ten years or more. It has never been demonstrated that these results are any better than no treatment at all. The report in 1970 by Segaloff (quoted by Nieper) showed that if radiation was used after breast surgery the relapse rate was just as high as in those patients who had no radiation. The only difference was that when the cancers did recur, there were more malignancies in vital organs among those who had received radiation. A recent Swiss investigation by Stjernswärd showed that premenopausal women who had received radiation after breast surgery had a shorter life expectancy than women who had no treatment at all.

The overall statistics[2] for survival of patients for five years after surgery for cancer of all types is in the region of 15 per cent. This is true if there has been no secondary growth at the time of surgery. If metastasis has occurred prior to surgery then statistically there is a survival rate of 0 per cent.

Bauer and Fischer[3] in 1949 analyzed 10,000 cancer cases and showed a 17.9 per cent survival rate over a five year period. Of these 10,000 nearly two thirds were cases of skin cancer.

An editorial in the *British Medical Journal* stated that women were still being subjected to major surgery even after the spread of the disease. Frequently patients were seen with dissemination of the disease a few months after pointless and mutilating surgery. Wilkinson[4] indicates that the relative swing away from radical surgery had less influence on the outcome than the innate biological characteristics of the tumour and the patient.

Dr Louis Goldman[5] firmly believes that cancer remains intractable. Surgical techniques, he maintains, have improved, more radical operations have been devised, useful (though not curative) anti-cancer drugs have been developed, undoubted advances have been made in the treatment of relatively unusual conditions such as Hodgkins disease and testicular tumours. Yet the result of treatment for common cancers of the bowel, breast and lung, which account for 70 per cent of cancer deaths, have remained unchanged for more than twenty years.

The statistical survival experiences of 400,000 white patients between 1949 and 1964 have been analyzed.[6] These were cases receiving current modes of treatment (surgery/radiotherapy/chemotherapy). There is a 60 per cent five year survival rate for patients with all types of cancer of the uterine cervix. This figure rises to 80 per cent if the disease is localized at the time of surgery. Stomach cancer provided a 14 per cent five year survival rate for women and 11 per cent for men. Lung cancer showed a 65 per cent five year survival rate for women and 51 per cent for men. Cancer of the colon, which is more frequent among women than men, gave a 47 per cent survival rate after five years for women and 42 per cent for men. These examples indicate the wide variation in success rates claimed for the various cancer sites.

Since the primary aim of surgical intervention is the total removal of all malignant tissue, it is obviously a great advantage to the surgeon if the area involved is discreet. For this reason localized areas of skin cancer are more successfully dealt with than an area of the body which is less accessible, such as the large intestine. Another area which lends itself to total removal is the female reproductive system. Tumours that develop on the cervix, or womb, and which have not spread to adjacent tissues or metastasied, lend themselves to surgical removal. This is not to say that the dietetic and supplemental methods advocated should be ignored, but merely to point out that some areas of surgical intervention are more likely to be successful than others by virtue of the anatomical position and physiological character of the tissues involved. Surgical techniques have no doubt been perfected in such surgical measures and further progress from a surgical point of view is unlikely.

Early Diagnosis

Much is made of the value of early diagnosis. To this end mass screening of women using the 'smear' test has been carried out. Other techniques such as mammography, thermography and mass X-Rays have also been used. But the yield of positive cases in such screening efforts is very low. Only about one in 500 to 700 of the people tested show positive signs of cancer development and many of these are already too advanced for treatment to be considered of likely benefit. Although tumours may be detected earlier by these methods, there is no convincing evidence that the chance of cure is really increased.

Professor Cochrane,[5] director of the Medical Research Council's Epidemiology Unit in Cardiff, points out that the death rate from cancer of the cervix was falling before smears were introduced and that it has gone on falling at the same rate in most areas since. There is no convincing evidence of a greater fall in the death rate from cancer of the cervix in those areas in which mass screening has been introduced. There is of course the reassurance factor, whereby women who have had the test and are passed as cancer-free feel a psychological release from the fear of cancer. A much cheaper method would be to educate the public as to the real causes of the pre-cancerous state and how to avoid it.

In many cases, of course, surgery must be considered essential to preserve life. Where a tumour threatens life, by impinging on a vital vein or artery, or where obstruction of the digestive tract is taking place, the intervention of the surgeon can often be life-saving. Of course this is unlikely to be a long-term solution and despite the psychological uplift to the patient at having the 'lump' removed, the outlook would remain grave without a concerted effort to attack the causes of the disease and to rebuild the shattered defence mechanism of the body, where this is possible.

The obvious dangers of surgery are further complicated, in cancer cases, by the inherent danger of spreading of the malignant cells. Any cutting of the tumour, even by biopsy, tends to result in the spread of such seed cells. The skill of the surgeon is of vital importance in that he must ensure, if at all possible, that he removes an intact, undamaged tumour. As Nieper so succinctly puts it, 'Surgical therapy is a short-term therapy as well as being topically limited.'

It is difficult to compare untreated cases with treated ones. The evidence that has been available has been correlated by Hardin B. Jones Ph.D., Professor of Medical Physics and Physiology at the University of California, Berkeley.[7] His findings were that there was no relationship between the extent of surgical treatment and the length of life expectancy in cases of verified malignant disease. Simple surgical excision was found to produce the same survival rate as the more radical surgical methods (referring to breast cancer). These findings correspond to similar reports in Britain.

In considering the general surgical treatment of cancer, Jones found that the apparent life expectancy of cases having had *no* treatment seemed to be greater than the treated cases. In order to arrive at this conclusion Jones had adjusted the statistical factors to take into account the fact that many long-term survivors were patients who had slow-growing tumours. These tended eventually to attract surgical intervention. By the very nature of the relatively benign state of their tumours they remained alive to boost the numbers of long-term survivors after surgery. By the same token these patients would probably have had long-term survival potential even if untreated. The opposite picture obtains for those suffering from highly malignant, quick-growing tumours. These cases might not be suitable for surgery as a result of rapid spread of the disease prior to the first medical contact being made, and such cases swell the figures of those who die untreated.

The statistical balance is therefore not a matter of simply comparing the survival records of those who undergo surgery and those who do not. It is the factors which lie behind the survival times that are important, not the intervention or otherwise of surgery.

The other statistical trick often used, albeit in innocence, is to combine the huge numbers of long-term survivors of skin cancers with the short-term survivors of other forms of cancer, in order to produce a longer 'average' life expectancy.

In discussing statistics it is worth examining a disquieting factor. In a report entitled *Accuracy of Certification of Cause of Death*,[8] the result of post mortems on over 9,000 patients in seventy-five British hospitals during 1959 were compared with the 'cause of death' described by the attending physician. In only 45.3 per cent of the cases was the cause of death, as described by the post mortem, in full agreement with that given at the time of death. The doctors in attendance tended to diagnose lung cancer and peptic ulcer less frequently than the pathologists. The report states that 'Only one quarter of deaths were associated with disagreement of fact.'

Now to have a 25 per cent difference of opinion as to fact may not seem too important to the reader; but a little reflection will show what havoc such mistakes can play with the accuracy of statistical evidence. If out of the tens of thousands of figures analyzed each week, in order to compile evidence for or against particular forms of treatment, a 25 per cent degree of error had to be allowed, the whole undertaking would become meaningless. The 'differences of opinion' were not trivial. In many cases the cause of death was put as cardio-vascular disease, when in fact the patient had died as a result of lung cancer. It is obvious that an elderly patient may be suffering from a variety of degenerative complaints, not excluding cancer. The problem in assessing medical statistics is that we never know to what extent unconscious bias or error of this type enters the picture.

The question of bias, or the doctor's expectancy, is an important one in considering the relative value of statistics. Since few diseases follow a precisely predictable course and since doctors and standards of care differ from one area to another, and since most doctors are biased towards expecting certain results or therapeutic effects, a properly designed trial becomes difficult to create because of the unwanted conclusions which are bound to result from these factors.

If cancer were purely a localized disease then surgery could be considered as the treatment of choice. But it is seldom localized and so must be considered at best a short-term answer to a critical condition, since it deals with results and not with causes.

Another aspect of the surgical treatment of cancer is the removal of various hormone-producing glands such as the ovaries, testicles, adrenals and pituitary. Certainly there is evidence that in some patients there is a short-lived improvement following such procedures. The patient is often, however, left a 'hormonal cripple' reliant on hormone preparations to stay alive. These drastic procedures seldom result in more than a short term improvement. Bauer (1949) showed that there was no difference in average life-span, between patients who refused surgery and those that elected to have surgery in cases of stomach cancer. However, he found that radical surgery, which included adjoining organs, shortens the survival period by 40 per cent to 50 per cent.

Radiotherapy

We should not of course consider surgical methods in isolation, since these techniques are frequently combined with the use of radiation therapy, either before or after surgery, or both. There are many different techniques used in radiation. There may be localized application or a general whole body application. Any number of methods, with varying degrees of exposure to X-Rays, are used in an attempt to damage and destroy as much of the malignant tissue as possible, without harming surrounding normal tissues.

Many tumours are not accessible to radiotherapy and many types of cancer are resistant to this form of treatment (e.g. lung cancer). As previously mentioned, Segaloff, has shown that the relapse and mortality rates are just as high as in non-irradiated patients, and that the later group suffered fewer secondary tumours affecting major organs.

Radiotherapy must be seen as a short-term therapy and is not able to deal satisfactorily with a long-term phenomenon. Radiation is, of course, a major causative factor of cancer and doses of the magnitude normally delivered to cancer patients must severely increase the risk of further malignant tissue changes occurring. Various unpleasant side-effects can also occur after radiation therapy. Severe irritation of the bladder and rectum is a frequent result. Fistulae can also develop in these areas and are extremely painful. After X-Ray treatment for cancer of the cervix spontaneous fractures can occur in the hip region.

Now obviously there are successes in the field of radiotherapy. Some conditions and some techniques will produce a better life expectancy for the patient. But the overall rationale of the use of a patently dangerous and life destroying technique runs contrary to one of the prime requisites of any form of treatment. Therapy should be free of side-effects and should not suppress the body's ability to defend itself. Radiation therapy does not pass examination on either of these counts.

As with so much of medical thinking in relation to cancer there appears to be an obsession with the size of the tumour. Many research reports bristle with mentions of 'reduction in tumour size'. Tumours are seldom the direct cause of death unless they interfere with a vital blood-vessel or obstruct the function of the body in some way, such as a bowel or bladder stoppage. Radiation usually succeeds in reducing the total size of the tumour, but it does not simply destroy cancerous cells. A tumour contains many normal cells, connective tissue and blood vessels and radiation will destroy these tissues more effectively than it will cancer cells. What may occur, therefore, is a reduction in size of the tumour but not necessarily a reduction in the *active cancer process*. There is, indeed, often a dramatic increase in the malignant activity of these remaining cells after radiation.

The white blood cells are our main 'soldiers' in the war with invading micro-organisms and foreign bodies. Radiation therapy does great damage to the tissues (such as the marrow of the long bones) that produce these cells. The ability of the body to fight the cancer is markedly reduced as a result, as is its ability to fight infection in general.

In a speech delivered to a National Cancer Conference in 1968 Dr Philip Rubin, then chief of the Division of Radiotherapy at the University of Rochester Medical School, stated that the clinical evidence and statistical data in numerous reviews proved that no increase in survival rates had been achieved by the addition of radiation. At the same conference Dr Vera Peters, of the Princess Margaret Hospital, Toronto, Canada, indicated that in breast cancer there had been no true improvement in the mortality figures over the previous thirty years, despite the technical improvement in surgery and radiotherapy during that time.

In an article in the *American Journal of Roentgenology* in August 1976 the following statement appears:[9] 'In many quarters the superiority of combination therapy (surgery and radiotherapy) is accepted as established dogma, and re-examination of treatment policies as heretical. Despite the confident air of this position a life-sparing effect, specifically attributable to the radiotherapeutic component of combination regimens, has not been proved.'

It cannot be put more clearly.

'Consensus Medicine'

That some physicians, surgeons and radiographers are now questioning the dogma of orthodox medicine is encouraging. The fact is, however, that there exists a strong tendency amongst medical practitioners not to 'rock the boat'. It has been called consensus medicine. Because 'it' is accepted by everyone else in the profession 'it' must be right. 'It' might be a theory, a method of treatment, a technique or anything else that, by virtue of common use, comes to be part of the accepted pattern of medical practice. 'It' may have no rational or logical place in the sane treatment of sick people and yet still continue to be accepted for decades.

There are examples at every turn. One might think of Electro-Convulsive Therapy (ECT) in the treatment of depression. There is no scientific reason for this treatment, which often produces disastrous personality changes in the patient. There is no clear understanding amongst its staunchest medical defenders as to *how* it is supposed to do what it is expected to do. All that is certain is that by passing an electrical current across the brain the patient often comes out of a depression. That this in no way deals with the *causes* seems unimportant to the proponents of E.C.T. The causes might be biochemical, or emotional and yet the expedient short cut is taken. Avoid the cause; ignore the patient's needs; dismiss the probability of recurrence (if causes are ignored, recurrence will remain likely); simply shock the brain into a new pattern of behaviour and, of course, deny the importance of after-effects. These often leave the patient in a vegetable-like state for months or years, with little or no memory of the past.

What has this to do with cancer? Nothing, except that it has everything to do with a particular medical way of looking at the question of health and disease. Short-term measures are paramount; causes are largely ignored and statistics can be used to show that 'consensus' medicine is doing its stuff. Heaven help the practitioner who steps out of line and openly attacks such thinking! He risks professional suicide. There are many medical practitioners who are unhappy about methods and the emphasis on expediency within their profession. Some change their own approach and this is only slightly frowned on by the profession. It is only when a public stand is taken that the wrath of orthodoxy is hurled at the heretic. We will discuss this phenomenon further when we deal with the Laetrile controversy in America.

Chemotherapy

Anti-cancer drug treatment called 'Chemotherapy' attacks both normal and cancer cells.[10] Most drugs used in this way will damage the ability of the body to produce red and white blood cells. Blood transfusions are often required, as are antibiotics, because of the reduction in the ability of the body to cope with infection.

A group of these drugs called, alkylating agents, interfere with the process of cell division. This is meant to slow down the rate of cancer growth. Of course normal cells also divide and these too will be interfered with. This can result in damage, for example, to the digestive system, the skin, hair (which often falls out) and the bone marrow. The ability of the body to respond to infection is thus markedly diminished. This means that any chance that the body had of attacking the cancer process itself is destroyed.

Another group of drugs used against cancer cells are the so-called anti-metabolites. These alter various vital chemical processes by reacting with enzymes. These drugs are not selective and will also damage normal cells. The side-effects are very often thought to be worse than the disease being treated. Some of these drugs are also used in cases of organ transplantation in order to stop the body from rejecting the new tissue. It is worth noting that as a result of such treatment, the incidence of cancer amongst patients who have had immuno-suppressive drug treatment, following organ transplants, is up to fifty times higher than average.

Other drugs used, all of which are highly toxic, may be plant extracts which also have an interfering effect on both cancer and normal cell division. These include vinblastine, vincristine, vinleurosine and vinrosidine. The side-effects of these include, hair loss, marrow damage, nerve damage, fever and liver damage.

We have constantly stressed the importance to the patient of maintaining a sound immunological defence mechanism. All these drugs will destroy this mechanism. Short-term improvement in terms of tumour size or the rate of spread of cancer, is a small prize to compensate for the destruction of the body's ability to fight back against the cancer process, or infection. In the long run this must result in an increase of cancer, rather than any chance of curing the disease. These drugs are highly toxic, and are capable of inducing cancer in healthy tissue. No more than palliative effects can be expected in patients. This in itself is not enough to justify the horrendous side-effects of the drugs. Chemotherapy is not claimed to be curative. An associate Professor of Medicine at Stanford University, Dr Saul Rosenberg, has said that despite palliation of symptoms there will be an inevitable relapse and recurrence of the disease. This usually results in changes in the drug programme and eventual failure to control the disease.[11]

Statistics published in support of chemotherapy are highly suspect. Because of the destruction of the body's defences a patient may well succumb to a mild infection and die of the complications. The cause of death in such a case might justifiably be given as pneumonia. It is not difficult to see how deaths from cancer may appear to be lower as a result of such confusion of facts. Dr James Watson,[12] who has won a Nobel prize, has accused the National Cancer Institute of America of gross inaccuracy in its press releases regarding cancer cures, and in a speech in 1972 Dr Charles Moertal,[13] of the Mayo clinic, admitted that only a small fraction of patients treated with anti-cancer drugs experienced any benefit and this was usually short-lived. The failure rate was put at 85 per cent and some patients, especially those with gastro-intestinal cancer, were said to have a better survival capability without any treatment at all.

The toxic potential of these anti-cancer drugs gives them a very short-term effectiveness. Even if they act against the cancer, as hoped for, the limit on their usefulness would be imposed by the damage to the host organism. Obviously drugs can be varied in type and intensity by using different combinations and strengths. However, the long-term effects will still call a halt to the proceedings, even if an apparent benefit to the patient, of a short term remission, has taken place. In many cases the life expectancy of the individual is markedly shortened.

Nieper[14] quotes the Swiss cancer specialist, Brunner, as stating that if, in bronchial cancer, the drug cyclophosphamide was to be administered, life expectancy would be shorter than without any treatment, Nieper himself states that chemotherapy often results in considerable additional suffering to the patient. Remission is often paid for with a final iatrogenic (medically caused) collapse of the system.

The benefits, if any, of this form of treatment are out of all proportion to the suffering and torment which result from it. Many physicians involved in its promotion must be aware of the truth of what has been stated in this chapter. Where are their voices?

The most helpful area of current medical research is that which is looking at methods of strengthening the body's defence mechanism. This is known as immunotherapy. This area of research will at last investigate that aspect so far ignored: the self-healing tendency that is the only reason for anyone ever recovering from any disease.

For the rest, medical research into cancer seems to be along lines that lead to a dead end. The methods being investigated are those which, it is hoped, will selectively destroy cancer cells and not damage the body. Researchers have ignored the fact that the body can do this unaided, if the raw materials are present and if its defence mechanism is intact. They ignore the obvious in the search for a non-existent 'cure'. When the breakdown of health has reached the point of active cancer the idea of a 'cure' becomes meaningless. The only way health can be restored is by allowing the body to play its defensive role, by detoxification and regeneration of the mechanisms for survival. It may be too late to overcome the cancer process but the quality of life can still be improved. Surely this is a better prospect than the drugged, maimed and irradiated future offered by orthodox medical science?

The treatment of disease, not excluding cancer, should never be more dangerous than the disease itself.

[1] Breast Cancer Symposium, *Breast Surgery Journal*, 1969.
[2] Figures taken from *Medical Tribune, California Medical Digest, British Medical Journal* and Herberger (*Treatment of Inoperable Cancer*), Harris (*Cancer: The Nature of the Problem*), and Richardson (*Laetrile Case Histories*).
[3] K. Bauer and W. Fischer, *The Cancer Problem*, 1949.
[4] J. Wilkinson, *The Conquest of Cancer*, Hart-Davis MacGibbon, 1973.
[5] Louis Goldman, *When Doctors Disagree*, Hamilton, 1973.
[6] 'End Results in Cancer', Report No 3, *Statistical Bulletin*, February 1969.
[7] H.B. Jones, address to the American Cancer Society, 1969.
[8] H.M.S.O., 1966.
[9] Morrow and Di Sala, 'The Role of Post-Operative Irradiation and the Management of Stage I Adenocarcinoma of the Endometrium'.
[10] P. Parish, *Medicines*, Penguin, 1976.
[11] S. Rosenberg, 'The Indications for Chemotherapy in the Lymphomas', 6th National Cancer Conference, 1968.
[12] In evidence before the California Assembly Committee of Health, May 1976. See Richardson, *Laetrile Case Histories*.
[13] Speech at the National Cancer Institute Clinical Centre, May 1976. See Griffin, *World Without Cancer*.
[14] H. Nieper, 'Experience with Non-Toxic Cancer Therapies', paper delivered to German Society for Medical Tumour Therapy, Baden-Baden, 1976.

8

Psychological Considerations

The nature of cancer is established in popular mythology as an incurable disease. People will avoid talking about cancer and, wherever possible, will avoid thinking about it. Even the tone of voice used in mentioning cancer bears witness to the potency of the subject. Seldom is the word used openly with a normal modulation of the speaking voice. Rather a hushed, almost awe-struck tone of voice, is heard, as though even talking about this disease involves a certain risk.

Medical propaganda, regarding the improvement of diagnostic and therapeutic measures relating to cancer, seems to many to be meaningless. There are few people who do not personally have experience of friends or relatives struck down by cancer. The majority of these have not been successfully treated, as the statistics testify.

Many medical practitioners are not interested in the subject of cancer. Few general practitioners believe that there is any hope of cure in the majority of cancer patients with whom they have to cope. The very nature of the disease has thus led to patients who, in the main, do not believe that they can recover and doctors who do not believe that they can offer more than palliation and general care.

It is no wonder, therefore, that many patients are not told the true nature of their complaint, lest the knowledge be too much for them to bear. To tell someone that their condition is 'terminal' or 'incurable' or 'inoperable' might well lead to an understandable state of resigned depression.

In order to be free of fear and negative emotion a calming of the mind is required. This might be achieved through psychotherapeutic counselling, religious experience, meditation, and so on. The acceptance of oneself, in a non-critical manner, and the acceptance of life as it is, can lead to the disappearance of self-pity.

As Krishnamurti[1] explains, 'There is the ending of fear, which means the ending of sorrow and the understanding of oneself — self-knowing. Without knowing oneself there is no ending of sorrow and fear. It is only a mind that is free from fear that can face reality.' The task that needs to be undertaken is one of re-education. Patients, their families and friends and their medical advisers all need to understand more clearly the nature of the disease and the potential that exists for recovery.

Whether the patient should be told the true nature of his or her condition or not must depend on the individual patient. Were the average individual possessed of a more hopeful picture of the prospects for recovery such a conspiracy of silence would be unnecessary.

It used to be thought that cancer had a more profound influence on the patient's state of mind than the psychological condition of the patient had on the development of the disease. It is now known that the personality and psychology of the patient has a profound effect on the course of the illness.

Herberger[2] notes that chronic anger, disappointment, fear and the inability to cope with misfortune all play a role in the development of cancer. A positive, hopeful determination can, by contrast, have a profoundly helpful effect on the disease. Herberger quotes the case of a young woman who had multiple secondary growths and yet under biological treatment had made remarkable progress. This progress continued until an unthinking visitor (an ex-nurse) had told her that her improvement was only temporary. Doubt and fear had a disastrous effect and the patient soon died. Such expressions as 'nothing can be done for you' or 'your case is hopeless' can be the very factor that seals the fate of the patient.

Remission and total regeneration occur more frequently than most doctors would care to admit. If the whole programme of treatment were aimed at just such a situation coming about, then a far more hopeful, supportive attitude could be adopted by the doctor. The patient who can accept the fact that he has cancer and who is determined to do those things necessary to recover health will stand a greater chance of succeeding than the patient who does not expect to recover and who is negative and pessimistic regarding the future.

Naylor[3] has analyzed the attitudes of patients with cancer.

The most significant correlation was found between cancer patients and an attitude to life which had no sense of the future. There were also indications of much dwelling on past bereavements; a general lack of confidence and need for psychological help. 'Having no sense of the future' showed itself only in conversation with cancer patients but not in talks with old and infirm patients, suffering from other diseases, who were able to 'look forward' in a natural manner.

The likelihood of a cure for cancer can be greatly assisted by a patient whose personality can be altered in such a way as to produce the ability to enjoy deep relaxation. The physician should cultivate the art of empathy. The patient must be instilled with faith in himself; a positive, hopeful anticipation of recovery through logical methods, cheerfulness and the serenity which maintains the body's strength to fight the cancer.

Methods such as meditation, bio-feedback, autogenic training, deep relaxation and yoga breathing techniques are all useful in therapeutic terms. The mind of the patient should be harnessed to the task of recovery.

The quality of life can be improved by adding the dimension of hope. Is this a false premise, since many may not recover? I believe that the injection of hope into the patient together with a positive programme of action, both dietetic and psychological, are the first therapeutic steps. The honest answer to the patient's question 'Can I recover' must be 'I very much hope so'.

Dr Carl Simonton,[4] Chief of Radiation Therapy at Travis Air Force Base in America, has evolved a successful psychotherapeutic method in assisting cancer. Having observed that some patients made excellent recoveries and others did not, he set out to analyze the psychological profiles of these two groups. He found that those who recovered generally possessed a more positive will to live and a more hopeful attitude towards the disease and life itself. After studying various techniques, such as autogenic training and 'mind control', he developed a technique which involved the patient in introducing a positive programme of mental imagery. Using simple relaxation techniques the patient is asked to set aside three periods of fifteen minutes each day, during which time he should adopt a mental image of his disease; his treatment; the way the body was interacting with the treatment and the disease; the positive image of his tumour disappearing and his body whole and well.

Results quoted by Dr Simonton are most encouraging. The

more co-operative and positive the patient, the better the results. The deeper the relaxation or meditation achieved, the better the results. Simonton's ideas have been well-received by those medical practitioners who have examined them. The technique requires the patient to be fully informed as to the nature of the disease and the role of the various therapeutic measures being used. The techniques of relaxation and/or meditation can be learned at various centres or by instruction from the physician.

Dr Thomas Harris[5] explains that man is a creature whose present situation is constantly dominated by his future. Thinking is not merely awareness of action, but is a true creative 'cause'. Something happens when we think which could not occur otherwise. This is known as self-causation. Man, therefore, is not only the result of his past but also the result of his anticipated future. For this reason hope and self-imagery must be seen as positive contributions, since they chain the vision of a positive future to an uncertain present.

Patricia Griffin R.N., the co-author of *Laetrile Case Histories*, mentions that there are certain categories of cancer patient where there is greater enthusiasm for the methods of treatment than average. These patients, she says, are more consistently faithful to all aspects of the regimen, including the diet. The success rate and long-term survival rate in this group are also markedly higher than average. These patients suffer from cancer of the prostate and Patricia Griffin postulates the theory that it is the drive to preserve potency in these patients that marks them as different. Were this drive as marked in all patients, she suggests, the survival rate would improve dramatically.

The will to live; a love of life; positive, cheerful serenity; a spiritual calm; mental imagery of recovery; hope for the future. These are the keys to the mental, complementary approach to the positive dietary methods already discussed.

Which is more important, the mind or the body? They cannot be separated, since they interact at each level of life.

We must never raise false hopes, but nor must we deny the reality and value of hope.

[1] J. Krishnamurti, *The Flight of the Eagle*, Servire Publishers, 1971.
[2] W. Herberger, *Treatment of Inoperable Cancer*, John Wright and Son, 1965.

[3] V. Naylor, *Emotional Problems of Cancer Patients*, Kershaw Press.
[4] C. Simonton, 'The Role of the Mind in Cancer Therapy', lecture at the University of California, 1972.
[5] T. Harris, *I'm O.K., You're O.K.*, Pan, 1970.

9

The Laetrile Controversy

The furore that has raged in America over Laetrile has been intense. Passions on both sides have been expressed violently. The effort, on the part of the 'establishment', to suppress the use of Laetrile and the slurs and slanders uttered by them, in this cause, are legion. The counter-attacks, by the proponents of Laetrile have been equally outspoken and critical. The motives of the authorities have been seriously questioned. Suggestions of dishonesty, corruption and even criminal intent have been levelled by both sides, against each other.

We shall attempt to identify the antagonists and try to examine some of the motives and truths that have emerged as a result of the confused and violent happenings of the past few years. Attempts by the Food and Drug Administration (F.D.A.) in America to have Laetrile banned have been carried out in co-operation with the American Medical Association (A.M.A.) and the National Cancer Institute (N.C.I.). In order to persuade public and medical opinion as to the uselessness of Laetrile a number of different tactics have been employed.

1. Laetrile has been stated to be worthless in the treatment of cancer. It has been said to have no cytotoxic (anti-cancer) effect. Tumours (of mice) have been said to be unaltered by its administration.
2. Laetrile has been said to be potentially dangerous because of its cyanide content.
3. The treating of people by the dietary regime advocated by the proponents of Laetrile is said to be 'quackery' and to be depriving patients of the chance of a cure via orthodox therapy.
4. Laetrile proponents are said to be 'cashing in' on the misery of others.

The various groups and individuals who have fought back against the bureaucratic attempt to stifle Laetrile therapy, can be classified as being under the umbrella of the Cancer Control Society (C.C.S), the National Health Federation (N.H.F.) and the Committee for Freedom of Choice in Cancer Therapy (C.F.C.C.T.). Their answer to these accusations is as follows.

Laetrile has never been adequately tested by any independent authority. Many clinical results from practitioners in the U.S.A., Mexico, Germany, Phillipines and Holland are ignored by the F.D.A. Where tests on human cancer patients have been carried out by the F.D.A., or other anti-Laetrile agencies, the dietary component has been ignored and doses of Laetrile have been too small. Despite this many patients reported subjective improvements, such as less pain, greater appetite and often a gain in weight. These benefits were discounted as being of 'no significance' by the authorities.

In tests on mice tumours the main criterion used is of reduction in tumour size. Laetrile is not a toxic drug. It does not burn or poison healthy tissue. The orthodox methods employed will, under test conditions, produce observable toxic effects on all tissues. Laetrile will only act against cancer cells by virtue of the presence of specific enzymes in and around these cells. A tumour mass (especially the type used in the transplanting of tumours to mice, for testing) comprises a relatively small quantity of actual malignant cells. Were conditions advantageous for Laetrile activity and all these cells were to be destroyed, there would still only be a small reduction in tumour size.

As long as investigators expect Laetrile to act in the same manner as the cytotoxic chemicals currently employed by orthodox medicine, so long will they fail to find what they are supposed to be looking for. In the many tests of this type the tumours exposed to Laetrile were either transplanted mouse tumours or cancer cells in culture dishes. The respiratory rate of such tumours is extremely low[1] and this does not favour Laetrile activity. The main criterion of increased life expectancy in living cancer patients has not been tested except by those in favour of Laetrile.

Many distortions and inaccuracies have come to light in analysis of the official tests, which the F.D.A. use, to show that Laetrile is 'useless'. What is more evident, on examination, is the lengths to which officialdom has gone to avoid testing the total Laetrile programme.

The suggested toxicity of Laetrile is a red herring. Enormous doses would have to be administered to produce any slight toxic reaction. Since all the current orthodox treatments are highly toxic and since many cancer patients, undergoing chemotherapy, die of iatrogenic (medically induced) collapse, such accusations can be ignored. Laetrile in recommended doses is totally non-toxic. The cyanide component is 'locked in' until the cancer tissue is reached and only cancer cells are then destroyed. Even doctors opposed to Laetrile acknowledge that it is as safe a compound as could be found.

The accusation that Laetrile therapy will divert patients from orthodox treatment, however, *is* valid. If a patient decides for himself that this is what he wants, having considered the arguments for and against, then surely that is his privilege. Most patients turning to Laetrile have had orthodox treatment, and have found themselves in a 'terminal state'. Since their survival prospects under orthodox care at this stage is 0 per cent, is it not reasonable to introduce hope into their lives and, in at least 15 per cent of these 'terminal' cases, to look for a normal life-span? To attract patients away from orthodoxy might create just the nudge needed to make the many dissatisfied medical practitioners look to new and better methods.

In Europe Laetrile is available at approximately 80p per gram (98 per cent extraction) and 50p per gram (65 per cent extraction). An average cost to the patient would be about £45 per month if they were taking 2 grams daily. If, as it should be, this were available on the N.H.S. it would cut the cost of care of cancer patients by up to 75 per cent.

The tactics employed by the F.D.A. in its attempts to enforce the ban on Laetrile are hair-raising. A study of the details is spelled out in a meticulous manner by G. Edward Griffin in *World Without Cancer*. The motives for such methods are not always easy to define. Certainly there are indications that money has played a part in the decision making. Vast research grants are made annually in America for cancer research. Sums of money running into thousands of millions of dollars, which fund projects employing hundreds of thousands of people, are involved. Much of this money is derived from the vast conglomerates which control the pharmaceutical and petrochemical industries internationally. The intricate intermeshing of F.D.A. officials, high ranking medical personnel, influential directors of research projects, executives of drug manufacturing corporations and the various organs of the mass media, is a complex but real fact. Many of these groups depend upon each other, and vast amounts of money hang on their decisions.

The drug manufacturers depend upon F.D.A. co-operation in the licencing of their products. The F.D.A. is staffed by the students of medical establishment training and former drug house executives. Research grants from the drug houses to various academic institutions is dependant upon the areas and directions of such research being clearly defined by the donors.

One of the world's great scientists, Linus Pauling, winner of a Nobel Prize, has been unable to attract major grants for his current research work. The reason? He is investigating orthomolecular medicine which, put in its simplest terms, means that he is interested in the substances people eat and the relationship between diet, health and disease. There is no money in this for the drug houses and therefore no money for Dr Pauling. Were he to announce an attempt to research the use of some product derived from petrochemicals, then he would have no problem in attracting funds.

The Pauling Institute was reduced in 1976 to placing an advertisement in the *Wall Street Journal* to solicit research funds. The advertisement included these words: 'Our research shows that the incidence and severity of cancer depends upon diet. We urgently want to refine that research so that it may help to decrease suffering from human cancer... the U.S. Government has absolutely and continually refused to support Dr Pauling and his colleagues here in this work during the past four years'.

What more poignant and telling commentary is necessary? One of the century's greatest minds, intent on solving one of the greatest challenges to mankind, with a begging bowl in his hands held out to the richest nation on earth!

Laetrile has nothing to offer the drug houses. It is relatively cheap and easy to extract from its many natural sources. There is no future in Laetrile for the research workers, most of the development has been done by Dr Krebs, who first announced its value in 1952. It is unlikely that funds would be available for such research.

There is more than fifteen thousand million pounds spent on cancer research, detection and treatment in the U.S.A. annually. The livelihood of hundreds of thousands depends upon the expanding industry surrounding cancer. In America more people live *off* cancer than die *of* it (350,000 annually at present). Is it then any wonder that Laetrile, with its emphasis on simplicity and based on diet, should attract the wrath and displeasure of those whose job it is to know what is best for the man in the street? What about the men and women working in these fields of research? Don't they want to find a cure for cancer? Are they not spurred on by the dream of helping to rid mankind of the scourge of cancer? Of course they are. But by the nature of their training and the areas of their enquiries they are bound to fail. As long as they are trying to find better ways to cut, burn or poison the body into a state of health, they will always fail. And there is little or no money available to research natural, simple, drugless therapy. So how can these dedicated and hard working scientists take Laetrile, enzyme therapy and diet seriously? They cannot break out of the mould in which they have been cast. Dr Simonton has described the effect of consensus thinking on a young physician:

> As I got further into medicine, I discovered that it was very difficult to help people in the way that I had hoped to help them. On every hand I was being shown that it was impossible, or at least nearly impossible, to make any major breakthroughs in the field of cancer research therapy. I am sure most physicians go through some degree of this when they find out that the good they are able to do is much less than they had hoped it would be. While the physician is under all the pressures of current concepts and limitations both from the system itself and the people who teach him, at the same time he feels a tremendous responsibility to make right decisions. He *must* always be right, for fear that in being wrong he may endanger someone's health or life. This fear causes him to accept the medical teachings that are given to him. He hesitates to think much on his own for fear his wrong thinking may cause further ill health or ultimately death on the part of the patient. This feeling is largely generalized in our thinking, and during these focal years we have a tendency to be very close-minded because of this tremendous, overwhelming fear.

If this is true for physicians and surgeons then it is true for research workers. No malicious, anti-humanitarian motivation need by ascribed to these people. Only simple fear of stepping out of line, fear of rejection by one's peers, fear of being attacked as a heretic.

Time magazine (25 July 1977) headlined a Senate subcommittee hearing on Laetrile 'Challenging the Apricot-Pit Gang'. The reader knows immediately who the 'bad-guys' are. The word 'gang' creates the tone of the piece. The report is sneeringly contemptuous of 'the Laetrile crew' who have the temerity to ask that clinical tests should include the dietary programme outlined in this book. After all, this is how Laetrile works. Why should it not be tested in the most advantageous manner? What is the use of testing only part of a system? Would a test on diabetic treatment ignore the dietetic component? But *Time* has its sneer. It even trots out the hoary old chestnut about Laetrile being potentially toxic: 'Dr Joseph Ross raised the "strong possibility" that long term ingestion of Laetrile could result in chronic poisoning similar to that from the starchy Cassava root, which like Laetrile, contains cyanide.'

We have already exposed the fatuous nature of this lie. Should more proof be required a report by Dr Oke of the University of Ife in Nigeria, entitled *The Prophylactic Action of Cassava,* shows that toxicity is rare and is dependent on a general deficiency in the diet rather than an inherent poisonous tendency of cassava.

Loaded emotionally against the advocates of Laetrile the *Time* article attempts a final laugh at the expense of Dr Ernst Krebs Jnr., the developer of Laetrile. Senator Ted Kennedy (whose own questionable past exploits are studiously ignored by *Time*) is shown as a knight in shining armour attacking this 'gang' of imposters: 'The only applause from the gallery was when Senator Kennedy wryly corrected Krebs, who had referred to the F.D.A. Commissioner as "Mr. Kennedy". Said the Senator (no kin): "He's Dr Kennedy. You are Mr Krebs". That was a pointed reminder to all the world that Krebs, who likes to call himself "Doctor", has only an honorary Ph.D.'. This is the level of smear to which *Time* and other journals are reduced. Krebs is a biochemist and his honorary doctorate entitles him to be so addressed.

A report in *The Observer,* 10 July 1977, headlined 'U.S. Row over Apricot "Cure" for Cancer', carried a slightly less hysterical, but nevertheless biased viewpoint. All statements from the F.D.A. and N.C.I. are carried as being sensible and sound. All mention of those in favour of Laetrile's use are treated with the usual smear tactics. Most are labelled 'faddists', which I suppose means that they are fussy about what they eat or what drugs they avoid taking. The leading lights such as Dr Richardson are mentioned in such a way as to cast doubts as to their reliability. 'Dr John Richardson, a leading member of the John Birch Society' and 'Dr Richardson recently lost his licence to practice in California for illegal use of Laetrile.'

Indeed Dr Richardson (Author of *Laetrile Case Histories*) might well be a member of a political group that seeks a radical change in American politics. (The John Birch society is a right wing organization.) He has been subjected to indescribable harassment and victimization by the F.D.A. His book is a testament to his spirit and should be read by all who wish to understand the struggle for the recognition of the value of Laetrile therapy.

His 'crime' for which he was tried, convicted and disbarred? No, not murder or rape or arson but smuggling. Again — not gold or diamonds or heroin — but Laetrile. The movement of Laetrile across inter-state borders is a Federal crime in the U.S.A. The F.D.A. has the power, and has used it, to stop doctors from obtaining Laetrile for their patients. A Doctor, knowing that Laetrile is harmless, can lose his licence to practice because of his dedication to the belief that his vow to help his patients is more important than bureaucratic double-think.

Justice has however prevailed. An informed public has pressured its state legislators to defy the F.D.A. Fourteen States have now legalized the use of Laetrile. Legislation is pending in twelve more. Inter-state restrictions however are still in existence as the F.D.A. desperately attempts to stop the importation of anything and everything used in the manufacture of Laetrile.

A report in the *Dallas Morning News,* dated 25 September 1977 by a writer, Ken McHam, elaborates on this. After explaining the intense lobbying between those for and against Laetrile the article goes on:

After a hearing that lasted until 2 o'clock in the morning, the House Committee voted 8-0 in favour of the bill. Within a week, the bill was on the floor of the House for debate. Within another week, the House had passed the bill to the Senate by a vote of 133 to 8.

Three weeks later, the Senate approved the bill by a vote of 27 to 3, and nine days later, the Texas Laetrile Bill was signed into law by Gov. Brisco.

So Texas has made legal the manufacture, distribution, prescription and use of Laetrile. A great victory for the people, for cancer sufferers for those who are now forced to flee the country to use the drug?

No. Pressure and intimidation from the F.D.A. continues to threaten those who would research, manufacture, distribute or clinically use the substance. A Houston-based biological research corporation searching for a more effective Laetrile-based compound refused comment for this article out of fear they would then be harassed by the F.D.A.

Individuals who have made plans to establish a Laetrile clinic in Dallas, headed by Dr Mario Sotto, the medical director of Clinica Cydal in Tijuana, refuse to discuss for publication any connection with such a project. The project may be abandoned out of fear of harassment by the F.D.A.

Perhaps the F.D.A. can continue to plug the dike by using its most far-fetched and diluted interstate commerce controls to intimidate any potential research, manufacture or use of Laetrile.

But perhaps the flood of public opinion is rising too fast for the F.D.A. to long maintain its 'stonewalling' techniques.

Laetrile legislation has risen from one state to 12 in a period of only one year, and general public ignorance of the existence of Laetrile has risen to general public interest in the controversy, during the same year.

And that, after all, is only what is being asked for by the supporters of Laetrile — the freedom to use and develop a promising approach to cancer therapy. All that has ever been asked is for an unrestricted search for truth — more research, more facts.

I have recently returned from Hanover, Germany, where the 'Eumetabolic' therapy practised by the outstanding German internist Dr Hans A. Nieper has thus far produced the longest, most continuous period of remission of the tumour — and the greatest hope that the remission will continue until I become one of the few lucky ones who kill the disease before it returns them the favour.

Like other cancer patients in similar situations, I hereby knock on any wood I can find. And like every other cancer patient I have met, each in his own way — I pray.

Mr McHam, aged twenty-seven, is a cancer sufferer, or at least he was. His condition was controlled by treatment, including Laetrile. Now after a course of treatment under Dr Nieper in Germany his condition appears to be stable. Dr Nieper states that he is cured. With 2,200 new cases of cancer diagnosed daily in the U.S.A. and 1,100 people dying of cancer daily in the U.S.A., the battle for freedom of choice has been joined.[2]

The accusations made by the F.D.A., N.C.I., A.M.A. and the media can and have been answered. In Europe there are many pioneering practitioners whose results are beyond anything previously achieved by other methods.

The first seminar on Laetrile, in the U.K. was held in

January 1978 in Worthing. The nucleus of a group of like-minded and dedicated practitioners now exists. These comprise osteopaths, naturopaths, medical practitioners and medical herbalists.

One of those attending was Dr Alec Forbes who has gone on to become medical adviser to the Bristol Cancer Help Centre as well as a founder of ANAC (Association for New Approaches to Cancer). These two organizations are both doing sterling work in the field of treatment as well as the promotion of the ideal of a non-toxic approach to cancer.

Another who came to the seminar to hear Dr Hans Moolenburgh, was Dr Dick Richards. He has actively promoted these same ideals in lectures, on TV and in his thought–provoking book *Topic of Cancer*. Others present that day have incorporated into their work the ideas and ideals presented by the genial Dutch doctor who gave so freely of his time and energy. It is through the efforts of these like-minded people that we are beginning to see a gradual improvement in the understanding of and treatment of cancer.

Laetrile is part of a complex therapeutic programme. Its availability in the U.K. is now restricted to prescription only. Those who would undertake the task of self-healing should realize that it is not an instantaneous miracle-cure. It is rather a slow transformation of body, mind and spirit, during which the symptoms of cancer are often checked and sometimes eliminated. Whether or not concentrated Laetrile is incorporated into the programme should not influence the eventual outcome, since B_{17}-rich foods can be used to provide some of this potentially valuable substance. A positive and determined intelligent adoption of the ideas incorporated in this programme of diet, supplements and psychological and spiritual endeavour provides the most positive opportunity for an end to cancer.

Laetrile on Trial
Continuing public pressure, and the unending controversy resulted, also in 1978, in an official trial being organized for the Laetrile programme. The National Cancer Institute, funded by U.S. Government money, agreed to arrange for what was hoped would be a definitive study. Did Laetrile work? Was it safe? At the very least a public airing of the conclusions of the trial should point to a resolution of the agonizing choice which

so many cancer patients were having to make. Should they accept their medical practioner's advice and undergo orthodox therapy or fly in the face of the establishment and try 'quack' methods.[2] Or, as so many have done, should they try to do both simultaneously with questionable results?

To the uninitiated a medical trial involving prestigious scientists should be above reproach. The choice of the N.C.I. as the organizer of the trial was therefore questionable. This agency had been in the forefront of anti-Laetrile activity and statements for years. The choice of Dr Charles Moertal as the leader of the team conducting the trial was even more extraordinary. He had for over 10 years been making statements against the use of amygdalin in the press and elsewhere. It was predictable therefore that from the outset the Laetrile trial would be at the best controversial and at worst unacceptable to those who held Laetrile to be efficacious. The final result showed it to be both controversial and to a great extent unacceptable.

The trial itself consisted of 178 patients with cancer being treated with Laetrile and its associated (metabolic) programme (diet, enzymes, vitamins etc). According to the official report [3] the majority of the patients were in good general condition before treatment. It also claimed that the pharmaceutical preparations of amygdalin, the dosage and the schedule were representative of the past and present Laetrile practice. Results, it stated, showed no substantive benefit in terms of cure, improvement or stabilization of cancer, improvement of symptoms related to cancer, or extension of lifespan. To add to this apparently damning conclusion it was stated that the hazards of amygdalin therapy were evidenced in several patients by symptoms of cyanide toxicity or by blood cyanide levels approaching the lethal level.

So, a highly reputable group of scientists, under the auspices of a National Institute and funded by the U.S. Government, conducting a large-scale trial, using apparently 'correct' methods, comes out with a damning result. Laetrile and its programme are not only ineffective but dangerous. It would appear to be a final footnote to just one more example of medical quackery. On the other hand, if stage by stage and conclusion by conclusion the whole picture is analyzed a quite remarkable picture emerges, which can be shown to substantiate rather than nullify Laetrile's claims, and to throw serious doubt on the impartiality of the whole exercise.

Dr Alec Forbes, medical advisor to the Cancer Help Centre in Bristol, has looked at the trial with a critical and experienced eye. He has written as follows:

If a fair trial of the effectiveness of a new cancer agent is to be made, the usual method is:

1. To use a known, widely used example of the medicament recommended by its experienced users.

2. To employ exactly the same protocol of dietary and vitamin additions recommended by its protagonists.

3. To test on people not previously treated by other methods. In cancer advanced cases would be selected, preferably all with the same common type of disease. Cancer of the bronchus is a good example.

4. To have controls who are not treated at all is essential, but wherever possible they should also seem to be given the same treatment — i.e. dummy injections and tablets of the same colour and shape should be given to the controls.

5. The person giving the treatment should not know whether he or she was giving the agent tested, or the placebo.

6. The person asking the results of treatment should also not know what each patient received and preferably be different from the person who gave the treatment.

7. The person who selects the patients for treatment and the control should aim at choosing randomly which of a matched pair of cases is treated and which is a control. In this way the controls and treated cases are approximately at the same age and stage of disease.

8. In cancer the main criteria selected for assessment should be.
   (a) The duration of survival from the diagnosis of the disease.
   (b) The change in size of any observable masses;
   (c) The quality of life assessed by an index based upon:
      mood assessment
      appetite
      mobility
      amount of pain killers taken etc.
   (d) the side effects should be noted.

A Typical 'Doomed Trial'
If a doomed trial is to be conducted, attention should be paid to seeing that:

1. A new version of the product should be manufactured for use in the trial especially if there is known difficulty with the stability problem. This will pass the purity, but will deteriorate on storage and be less effective and more toxic.

2. Do not follow the recommended dietary and vitamin

programme of those experienced in the use of the agent to be tested, but make a show of doing so.

3. Select cases that have been previously thoroughly treated by other methods. This makes sure that they will respond little if at all to further treatment because their immune systems will have been damaged and bodies mutilated by operations.

4. Select cases with large lumps of cancer about them and with liver secondaries, they seldom survive long.

5. Have no controls.

6. Choose especially depressed cases for treatment.,

7. Give the patients being treated no emotional support and tell them their situation is hopeless.

8. Ensure the persons who administer the agent under trial have no experience of, or faith in, the substance, and that they do the assessment of the results.

9. Make the write-up of the paper, and especially the press release, condemnatory in tone. Omit all references to previous publications that show it works and is harmless if properly used.

Bearing these points in mind I would summarize the faults of the trial as follows:

The trial can be criticized for:

1. Being prejudiced from the outset.
2. Selecting patients with almost no chance of a positive response.
3. Not using Laetrile itself, but a similar substance.
4. Applying the wrong criteria to determine the benefit of Laetrile.
5. Not following the accepted course of Laetrile injections of fully observing the accompanying diet and supplement programme.
6. Discontinuing the injections too soon, when the majority of patients were 'stable'.

Indeed critics of NCI have gone so far as to call the trials 'rigged'. Whether this claim can be justified remains to be seen. What is certain is that the trials leave much to be desired. The very choice of the hostile N.C.I. to conduct the trials — not even ostensibly independent — is open to question.

The 178 patients selected for the trial were all dying, or to use the scientific term, they were 'phase IV' patients. To quote from NCI: 'All patients had proven cancer, beyond any hope of cure or therapy known to extend life expectancy.'

Thus, from the outset Laetrile was being asked to produce results on patients with such advanced cancer that no treatment could be expected to help. Usually early state cancer patients are selected for drug studies, i.e. those who have some hope of response. But not in this case! Why not? The next major question is whether Laetrile was actually tested. Without becoming too technical it is clear that Laetrile (i.e. laevo-amygdalin, as specified in the Merck Index) is quite different from the racemic amygdalin used in the trials. This is a less potent form of the compound, comprised largely of the by-products of its manufacture.

Dr Hans Nieper, Director of Silbersee Hospital, Hanover, says: 'The limited number of types of cancer selected for study, as well as the omission of necessary additional measures, the far too short observation periods, and the undefined chemical properties of the amygdalin form of mandelonitrile employed (Laetrile), all contribute to the devaluation of these efficacy tests, and the conclusions that can be drawn from them.[4] Why was real Laetrile not used?

The medical experts conducting the tests did modify the dietary pattern of the patients, but quite inadequately. Whereas animal protein, refined products, etc., were 'restricted', they were not banned from the diet, as they would have been by a Laetrile practitioner. Also wholefoods, fresh fruit and vegetables were 'encouraged', but not obligatory. This makes a total nonsense of the claim by the N.C.I. that 'all patients were placed on a diet identical to that currently recommended by most Laetrile practitioners'. Why was this?

Despite all these shortcomings, which also include inadequate vitamins, minerals and enzymes to accompany the Laetrile, there are indications that patients became stable in many cases. N.C.I. states that after three weeks of daily Laetrile injections (Recall that this was a substandard Laetrile derivative), well over half of the patients stabilized. In their terminology 'stable', means that these advanced, proliferating cases were no worse after twenty-one days (and equally they were no better). Instead of allowing the injection programme to run on for the usual three months or so of gradually diminishing injections, they were stopped at this point — *after just three weeks.* Why?

Normally Laetrile injections start with injections five or six times weekly for a month, then in the second month three times a week. The injections are then given twice weekly for the last month, with a continuing weekly maintenance dose thereafter. How could the NCI claim to be reproducing the normal practice when they abandoned injections, of substandard Laetrile, after so short a trial? The oral form of laetrile given thereafter was also of questionable quality.

The trial report mentions some cases of toxicity after its employment. As Dr Nieper states: 'The side-effects reported with only three doses of 500mg of amygdalin daily (orally) suggests that the toxicity was caused by impurities. The reported blood cyanide levels and other body effects are ordinarily *never observed* at this dosage.' Once again 'real' Laetrile was not being used. Why?

The Journal of the American Medical Association 13 February 1981, 254: 591—594 reported on Laetrile's lack of toxicity. There is no longer any doubt of its effectiveness against cancer among those who look objectively at the evidence. Recent animal tests at the Pasteur Institute in Paris show efficacy — and no toxicity. Unfortunately the trials in the U.S.A. were conducted by scientists hostile to Laetrile, and this prejudice was not hidden.

NCI's main criteria for improvement was the usual one of reduction in tumour size. But this is not the main goal in advanced cases. As far as the U.S. Supreme Court is concerned, any substance is effective if it provides pain relief, extension of life or a sense of well-being. These criteria were not assessed in these trials. And, in the words of Dr Nieper, 'It is certainly true that the cancer problem cannot be solved with mandelonitrile (Laetrile) derivatives, alone, but they are clearly helpful when employed in appropriate dosages.'

A further insight into the background to the trial has been made by Dr Dick Richards who states:[5]

To be of value, such trials should be conducted by above-suspicion fund sources. Cases must have had no chemotherapy or radiotherapy, both of which must impair unorthodox methods by limiting or preventing immune system response.

"It is not unknown for a board member of the American Cancer Society to also be a vice-president of a major food company. The chairman of the board of the Sloan-Kettering Institute, a leading orthodox cancer therapy centre, was also a director of a major pharmaceutical laboratory.

"The NCI discussed the toxic symptoms and other side-effects resulting from amygdalin. But there is no comparison with the atrocious side-effects of chemotherapy. What is more, in the U.S. Registry of Toxic Effects of Chemical Substances 1976, amygdalin falls between Class 1 (practically non-toxic) and class 2 (slightly toxic). Cytotoxic drugs are in class 6 (super toxic).

"The study purports to emulate the unorthodox programmes of therapy by using a diet and large doses of vitamins too. Yet it utterly excludes comment on preventive as opposed to therapeutic values. It also excludes the vital emotional/mental support techniques that must be used.

"All in all, this study well deserves to be included in the list of N.C.I. fund scandals. As a learned contribution to medicine it is at best, useless, and at worst of questionable integrity.

In a preface (entitled 'Closing the Book on Laetrile') to the official report in *The New England Journal of Medicine,* Arnold S. Relment M.D. suggests that Laetrile has had its day in court. This is not accepted by virtue of the criticisms of the manner of the choice of patients; type of Laetrile employed; partial use of associated therapy; bias on part of conducting team, etc.

Dr John Richardson who has strongly criticized the trial sums up the differences in approach as follows:[6] 'They think of the tumour as the disease. They are not paying any attention to the good results they got, such as the subjective improvement the patients experienced.' Though Richardson disagrees with the approach of the N.C.I. test, he softened his criticism toward physicians who treat cancer as a tumour disease. 'This isn't necessarily an evil approach', he explains. 'It's just their way of training. It's what they've learned. We don't look at cancer that way. We look at it as a chronic metabolic disease that has its resolution in the food we eat, and that can be prevented. It's really a condition involving the whole body. The tumour is just the symptom.'

Richardson points out, however, that metabolic therapy will have very little effect on a patient already subjected to heavy doses of chemotherapy and other toxic treatments. He also reiterates the basic difference in the function of amygdalin in the healing process and toxic therapies. 'It's a different world we're talking about,' he maintains. 'We're talking about a preventative. They're talking about people who have had everything destroyed... their enzyme system, their vitamins, their ability to eat and perform... all destroyed, and they are trying to see if a little apricot seed will dissolve a tumour.'

No doubt further trials will be undertaken for, far from damping down enthusiasm for the use of the Laetrile programme, the trial has fueled the controversy even more. Nor has the 'legalization' of Laetrile been affected. Shortly after publication of the report of the trial two more states, Missouri and West Virginia, aproved legislation legalizing its use. This brings the total to 25 states where Laetrile's use is legal. A nationwide Harris Poll showed that the public favoured the use of Laetrile in treating cancer by a 30 per cent margin.

1983 — The Year B_{17} Became a U.K. Issue

After five peaceful years during which a dramatic change took place in the minds of many practitioners in their attitude towards cancer, and during which time thousands of cancer patients were guided to a 'gentler' approach to the treatment of their disease, a political 'scare' was created over the free availability of B_{17}. The programme of diet, supplementation, psychological reorientation and visualization had been safely followed by thousands of patients in the U.K. Anyone who saw the BBC2 TV series of programmes entitled *A Gentle Way With Cancer* will have realized just how revolutionary an approach to cancer this whole package represents. One small but significant part of this was the use of Laetrile (B_{17}).

In over 250 cases of cancer with which I have been associated, all of whom have used B_{17} (as part of the whole programme) not a single one had side-effects as a result, or came to harm through its use. The same experience is true of all the practitioners of whom I know, who employ B_{17} as part of their treatment of cancer.

In the U.K., B_{17} has been freely available with the knowledge of the D.H.S.S. since 1978, but in 1982 Mrs Gwynneth Dunwoody M.P. started the controversy again by tabling questions in Parliament regarding the free availability of B_{17} and its possible toxicity. The press took up the hunt with headlines such as 'Banned "danger drug" Sold as Health Food' (*Mail-on-Sunday* 23 January 1983). The article stirred up public disquiet, even though the D.H.S.S. stated unequivocally that, to their knowledge, no harm had come to anyone in the U.K. as a result of taking B_{17}. The matter was then referred to the Committee for the Safety of Medicine for consideration. At this stage I personally sent 150 pages of evidence to Mrs Dunwoody. I asked her to read it and forward it to the Committee for their information. I pointed out that the evidence showed that, without doubt, pure Laetrile was virtually non-toxic, and effective.

In March 1983 the Health Food Manufacturer's Association took an extraordinary decision. They advised health stores to stop selling B_{17}. This organization had taken no evidence from supporters of B_{17} or from practitioners with experience of its use, or even from the suppliers and manufacturers of B_{17}. Thus, encouraged by the fact that there would be no resistance from a potentially powerful quarter, the D.H.S.S. on 28 March issued the following notice:

MEDICINES ACT 1968. PROPOSAL TO RESTRICT AVAILABILITY OF PRODUCTS CONTAINING AMYGDALIN (B_{17}, LAETRILE)

1. Amygdalin is a naturally occurring substance in plants, found especially in the kernels of apricots, peaches, and plums. When taken orally it is partially converted to cyanide by means of enzyme activity within the human body, especially in conjunction with other foods.

2. The amount of amygdalin in a single fruit kernel is very small and gives no cause for concern. But amygdalin is also currently on sale apparently as a health food supplement (under names such as 'Vitamin B_{17}') in the form of tablets or capsules containing substantial quantities of the substance. Where these products are not being marketed ostensibly for any medical purpose, they fall outside the present scope or control of the Medicines Act.

3. Amygdalin has, over the years, been widely publicized in the U.S.A. (under many different trade names, including Laetrile) and to a lesser extent in this country, as an unorthodox treatment for cancer. It seems reasonable to assume that many purchasers of amygdalin have this particular purpose in mind, since it has no apparent nutritive value.

4. The Committee for the Safety of Medicines was recently asked to advise on the safety of products containing amygdalin. The Committee's conclusion was that the evidence of potential risks to the general public was such that these products should no longer be available for purchase over the counter as 'health food supplements'. The Committee was also of the view that there was no evidence to support the efficacy of amygdalin in the treatment of cancer. Nevertheless if a doctor believed that, in the case of a particular patient and taking account of the risks, the substance should be prescribed then it should be brought within the ambit of the Medicines Act and should be available only in pharmacies under prescription. Such products should however not be licenced under the act.

The D.H.S.S. circular then continues to spell out the proposed legislation under which these proposals would become law. Thus, B_{17} has become a substance which, although essentially non-toxic, can only be obtained by prescription in the U.K. Thankfully it was not banned, and since a number of medical practitioners do advocate its use it will continue to be available to those most in need. The lack of organized opposition to this action is in marked contrast to the pattern in the U.S.A. where public pressure has achieved a reasonable level of availability of B_{17} for cancer patients in the majority of the states. It is to be hoped that a 'grass-roots' revolution of a similar kind will pressure the D.H.S.S. into revising its opinion and, at the very least, conducting a genuine trial of B_{17}.

[1] H. Nieper, 'A Medical Approach to Low-Toxicity Cancer Treatment of Long-Term Ambulatory, Hospitalized and "Incurable" Patients'.

[2] *Organic Consumer Report,* Vol 57, No 35, August 1977.

[3] Moertal et al, 'A Clinical Trial of Amygdalin — Laetrile in the Treatment of Human Cancers', *New England Journal of Medicine,* 28 Jan 1982, 306: 201—6.

[4] *Cancer News Journal,* Vol 16, No. 3 and 4 (1981 and 1982).

[5] R. Richards, letter to the Editor, *Times Health Supplement* 1981.

[6] J. Richardson, Press Release, July 1981.

Glossary

Amino-acid	The building material from which protein is made by the body.
Benign	When used in connection with a tumour it means one that is slow-growing and which does not metastasize and which therefore does not threaten life.
Biopsy	The removal, during life, of tissue to establish diagnosis.
Carcinogenic	Cancer-producing.
Catalyst	A substance which by its presence speeds up or slows down a chemical reaction but which remains unchanged by the process.
Chemotherapy	Treatment of disease by chemical drugs.
Cholesterol	A normal constituent of all animal fats and oils.
Cirrhosis	Chronic progressive disease of the liver.
Detoxification	A process whereby substances foreign to the body are changed to compounds more easily eliminated. Popularly thought of as 'cleansing' of the body.
Differentiation	Specialization of cells which takes place as the embryo develops.
Embryo	The product of conception, up to the third month of pregnancy.
Enzyme	A catalytic substance formed by living cells and having a specific action in promoting chemical changes.
Fermentation	The breakdown of complex substances under the influence of enzymes or ferments.
Fistulae	Opening of a wound or abscess, usually transmitting pus or fluid.
Glycolysis	The breakdown of carbohydrate in tissue to

	pyruvic or lactic acid; the means whereby cancer cells obtain energy when they no longer use oxygen.
Hormone	Specific chemical product of an organ which has regulatory effects upon remote tissues.
Hyperthermic	Therapeutic high temperature. Often induced by hot baths.
Iatrogenic	Usually means damage produced by the physician (or by drugs).
Immuno-suppressive	Treatment by drug or radiation which suppresses the body's defence mechanism.
Immuno-therapy	Treatment to help the efficiency of the body's defence mechanism. Usually meaning some form of vaccination.
Intravenous	Into a vein.
Leukocyte	White blood cell.
Lymphatic	To do with lymph, the fluid of the lymphatic system.
Macrophage	A cell which has the ability to attack and digest foreign organisms. Not a white blood cell.
Malignant	When used in connection with a tumour it means one that is quick-growing with undifferentiated cells and which may metastasize.
Mammography	The X-ray of a breast after the injection of a dye.
Melanoma	A tumour containing the black pigment melanin.
Metabolism	The complex phenomenon whereby the body assimilates food into tissue elements (anabolism) and breaks down complex substances into energy (catabolism).
Metastasis	The transfer of the site of a disease by means of cells travelling via blood or lymph.
Mitosis	The division by stages of a cell into two new cells.
Molecule	The smallest quantity into which a substance can be divided and still retain its characteristic properties.
Monocyte	A large leukocyte with one nucleus.
Organic	Having, or characterized by, organs; pertaining to living substances, as opposed to inorganic, non-living substances.
Pharmacological	Literally, to do with drugs; the action of a drug.

Proteolytic	Protein-digesting.
Protoplasm	The material forming the essential substance of the living cell upon which life depends.
Psychotherapeutic	Treatment using the mind and suggestion.
Radical surgery	The opposiste of conservative; in other words, drastic.
Radiotherapy	Treatment by X-rays.
Retro-transportation	Taking back from whence it came.
Thermography	Diagnosis by photographing the heat discharged by tissues. Infra-red radiation differs between normal and diseased tissue.
Toxic	Poisonous.

Further Reading

Getting Well Again, Dr O. Carl Simonton, Stephanie Mattews-Simonton and James L. Creighton, Bantam Books, 1980.
World Without Cancer, G. Edward Griffin, American Media, 1974.
Does Diet Cure Cancer? Dr Maud Tresillian Fere, Thorsons, 1971.
A Gentle Way With Cancer, Brenda Kidman, Century, 1983.
Cancer Therapy: Results of Fifty Cases, Max Gerson, Dura Books.
The Cancer Prevention Diet, Michio Kushi and Alex Jack, Thorsons, 1984.
Greek Vegetarian Cooking, Alkmini Chaitow, Thorsons, 1982.
The Four Seasons Wholefood Cookbook, Susan Thorpe, Thorsons, 1983.
Simply Delicious, Rose Elliot, Fontana, 1977.
Food for a Future, J. Wynne-Tyson, Centaur, 1979.
Nutrition and Health, Sir Robert McCarrison, The McCarrison Society, London.

General Information

For information of practitioners using alternative non-toxic methods in the treatment of cancer in the U.K. contact:

The Association for New Approaches to Cancer,
231 Kensal Road,
London W10.
(Tel. 01-969 1684)

The Cancer Help Centre,
Grove House,
Cornwallis Grove,
Clifton,
Bristol,
BS8 4PG.
(Tel. 0272 743216)

Gerson Therapy,
5 Village Grove,
Belsize Lane,
London NW3.
(Tel. 01-794 5823)

Cancer Control Society,
2043 N. Berendo Street,
Los Angeles,
California 90027,
U.S.A.

Suppliers of supplements including orotates, bromelaine enzymes, emulsified vitamin A etc:

Larkhall Laboratories,
225 Putney Bridge Road,
London SW15.

Most Health Food Stores stock suitable minerals and vitamins and some also carry stocks of papaya and pineapple enzymes. Other enzymes are obtainable from chemists.

The following societies promote correct nutrition:
The Vegetarian Society of the United Kingdom,
Parkdale,
Dunham Road,
Altrincham, Cheshire.

The Vegan Society,
47 Highlands Road,
Leatherhead,
Surrey.

The British Naturopathic and Osteopathic Association,
Frazer House,
6 Netherhall Gdns,
London NW3.

Magazines promoting correct nutrition include:
The Vegetarian (from the Vegetarian Society, above)
The Vegan (from the Vegan Society, above)
Here's Health, (from all Health Food Stores)
Healthy Living, (from all Health Food Stores)
Grace,
736 Christchurch Road,
Boscombe,
Bournemouth, Dorset.

Cancer Control Journal,
2043 N. Berendo Street,
Los Angeles,
California 90027, U.S.A.

Information on organic gardening and farming:
Henry Doubleday Research Association,
20 Convent Lane,
Bocking,
Braintree,
Essex.

The Soil Association,
Walnut Tree Manor,
Haughley,
Stowmarket, Suffolk.

Organic seeds can be obtained from:
Chase Organics,
Gibraltar House,
Shepperton,
Middlesex.

Wyatt Seeds,
Stone Cottage,
Beyton,
Bury St Edmunds,
Suffolk.

Information on suppliers of organic produce:
Organic Growers Association,
Aeron Park,
Llangeitho,
Dyfed,
Wales.

Information on all vegetarian sources of supply, guest houses,
publications, restaurants, organic growers, etc:
International Vegetarian Health Food Handbook.
The Vegetarian Society,
Parkdale,
Dunham Road,
Altrincham, Cheshire.

Index

vegetables, cooking of, 58,107
  growing of, 57
vitamins, 33,50,51,55,57–9,109,
    138,141,143
  A, 48,59,60,72,73,75,107
  B₁, 73,75,76,107
  B₂, 59,73,75,76,107
  B₃, 75,76,107,108
  B₆, 59,73,75,76,107
  B₁₂, 39,75,76
  B₁₃, 75,76,108
  B₁₅, 75,76,107
  B₁₇, 7,13,34,43,46,47,51,57–61
    74–6,79,80,82–4,103,137,
    144–6

C, 48,59,71,73,74,75,76,106
E, 59,73,74,75,76,106
K, 59
pantothenic acid, 107
sources, 75–6

Walker, Dr Kenneth, 18
Walker, M., 73
Warburg, 106
Watson, Dr James, 122
Wilkinson, J., 22,113
Williams, Dr Roger, 71,77
Wynne-Tyson, J., 56

X-Rays, 16,17,114,117